Teach Yourself VISUALLY™

Color Knitting

Teach Yourself VISUALLY™
Color Knitting

Mary Scott Huff

WILEY

John Wiley & Sons, Inc.

Library of Congress Control Number: 2012934991

ISBN: 978-1-118-06685-0 (pbk)

ISBN: 978-1-118-22242-3, 978-1-118-23634-5, 978-1-118-26103-3 (ebk)

Printed in the United States of America

10 9 8 7 6 5 4 3 2

Book production by John Wiley & Sons, Inc., Composition Services

Updates to this book are available on the Downloads tab at this site: http://www.wiley.com/WileyCDA/WileyTitle/productCd-1118066855.html. If a Downloads tab does not appear at this link, there are no updates at this time.

Credits

Acquisitions Editor
Pam Mourouzis

Project Editor
Suzanne Snyder

Copy Editor
Marylouise Wiack

Technical Editors
Karen Frisa and Rita Greenfeder

Editorial Manager
Christina Stambaugh

Vice President and Publisher
Cindy Kitchel

Vice President and Executive Publisher
Kathy Nebenhaus

Interior Design
Kathie Rickard
Elizabeth Brooks
Cheryl Grubbs

Photography
Matt Bowen

About the Author

Mary Scott Huff is the author of
The New Stranded Colorwork. She fled
the realm of information technology to
pursue a more yarn-centered
existence. The many friends she
found there have helped her become
a nationally recognized designer,
teacher, and author. A native of the
Pacific Northwest, Mary shares a wee
little house there with her husband,
two children, some Scottish Terriers,
and more yarn than is strictly necessary. Follow Mary's adventures playing
with string on her blog at www.maryscotthuff.com.

Acknowledgments

The author wishes to thank Linda Roghaar, Pam Mourouzis, Suzanne Snyder,
Matt Bowen, Karen Frisa, Rita Greenfeder, and the staff at John Wiley & Sons,
Inc. for their help and encouragement throughout this project.

This book is dedicated to Phillip, Lindsay, and Campbell Huff. You are the
brightest crayons in the whole box.

Table of Contents

Table of Contents

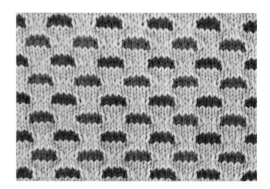

Table of Contents

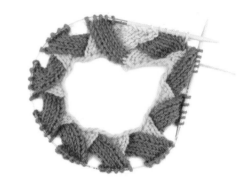

CHAPTER 1

Why Knit in Color?

Color is the ultimate expression of our personal selves in knitting. You can knit the same sweater as your best friend, making the same size, using the same yarn and needles. The colors you each select for your sweater are what give you two distinctly different and self-expressive garments.

The colors you choose for your knitting determine the mood of your work and the impact of each piece. Color can also be used to highlight areas you want to draw attention to and downplay or disguise those you don't.

Color, and the techniques employed to to highlight it, personalizes your work more than any other design choice.

Understand Color Relationships

The 12-part color wheel illustrates the ways that colors relate to one another, and helps you experiment with different combinations.

Color Wheel Relationships Explained

Working with a color wheel is a great way to kick-start your creativity when thinking about the colors you will choose for your knitting. In addition to showing the relationships between colors, the wheel also allows you to see the difference between different values and saturations of the same hue.

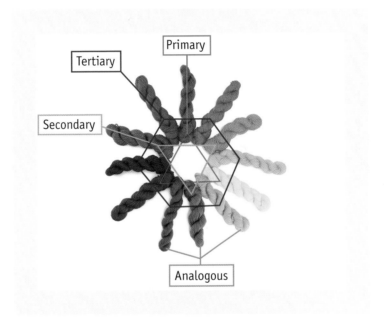

Primary: Red, yellow, and blue; these are the colors from which all other colors are mixed.

Secondary: The colors resulting from any equal-part mixture of two primaries: combine yellow and red to get orange, yellow and blue to get green, and red and blue to get violet.

Tertiary: The result of a mixture of a primary and the secondary next to it.

Analogous: Any group of three colors adjacent to one another on the color wheel.

Complementary: Colors that are opposite one another on the wheel. Violet and yellow, blue and orange, and red and green are reliably pleasing combinations.

HUE

Hue is the word used to describe the colors we see, expressed in color names. "Blue" describes a hue.

SATURATION

Saturation is an expression of the intensity (lightness or darkness) of a hue. The ball on the right could be described as "dark blue."

VALUE

Value describes the degree to which a color is diluted with white, gray, or black. Mixing a color with white creates a tint. Combining a color with gray creates a tone. Blending a color with black creates a shade.

TEMPERATURE

Temperature conveys the warmth or coolness of a color. Red, orange, and yellow (top row, above) are described as "warm," while green, blue, and violet (bottom row, above) are called "cool."

Rainbow Reptiles Project

Explore combinations from the color wheel by knitting a rainbow of reptiles.

Meet the Rainbow Reptiles

Pete, a Primary Python: Pete's red, yellow, and blue stripes may remind you of kindergarten (is that why they call it Primary School?), but he still has something to teach. The colors Pete wears are where it all begins. All the other colors in the world are based on some combination of Pete's stripes.

Sam, a Secondary Serpent: Sam sports secondary stripes. His orange, green, and violet bands are equidistant from the primaries on the color wheel. Secondary colors are equal mixes of any two primary colors.

Tim, a Tertiary Taipan: Tim is wearing a combination of tertiary colors, which are made by mixing a primary with the secondary next to it. Think of tertiaries as the colors "in between."

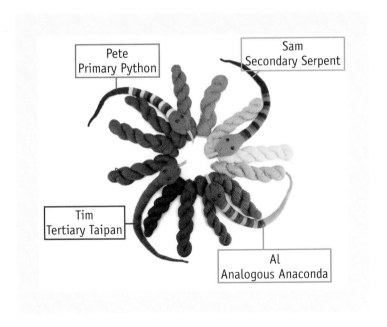

Al, an Analogous Anaconda: Al wears yellow-green, green, and blue-green. These colors are adjacent to one another on the wheel, and are of the same temperature. Analogous colors seem to flow into one another, due to their proximity on the wheel.

Specifications

SIZE
Finished measurements: 2½" wide × 17½" long

YARN
Fingering-weight yarn

Shown: Simply Socks *Sock Yarn,* 80% superwash wool, 20% nylon; 175 yd./50g skein. 1 skein each: #200 Cherry Red, #357 Orange, #430 Buttercup, #515 Fiesta Lime, #550 Green, #580 Teal, #650 Blue, #710 Blue Violet, and #215 Magenta

NEEDLES
Size 2 (2.25mm) DPNs, or size needed to achieve gauge

OTHER MATERIALS
2 oz wool roving or other stuffing

Eight ¼" buttons

½ yd. ⅜" grosgrain ribbon

Tapestry needle

Stitch marker

Sewing needle and thread

GAUGE
34 sts and 48 rnds = 4" in St st

Pattern Stitches

Stripe Pattern: *6 rnds B, 6 rnds C, 6 rnds A; rep from * for patt, ending with 6 rnds B.

Pete, Primary Python: A: Cherry Red, B: Buttercup, C: Blue

Sam, Secondary Serpent: A: Orange, B: Green, C: Blue Violet

Tim, Tertiary Taipan: A: Magenta, B: Blue Violet, C: Teal

Al, Analogous Anaconda: A: Teal, B: Green, C: Fiesta Lime

Knit the Rainbow Reptiles

SERPENT'S HEAD

1. With DPNs and color A, CO 30 sts. Join for working in rnds, being careful not to twist. Work 3 rnds in St st, PM after 15 sts.

2. Inc rnd: K2, M1L, work to 2 sts before M, M1R, k4 (slipping M), M1L, work to last 2 sts, M1R, k2. Work inc rnd every 3rd rnd 4 more times—50 sts.

3. Work 8 rnds even.

4. Dec rnd: K1, ssk, work to 3 sts before M, k2tog, k2, ssk, work to last 3 sts, k2tog, k1. Work dec rnd every 3rd rnd 4 more times—30 sts. Work 1 rnd even.

STRIPED BODY

1. Change to color B and work 3 rnds in stripe patt. Dec rnd: K2tog, work to M, k2tog, work to end of rnd.

2. Cont in stripe patt, working dec rnd every 18th rnd 4 more times—20 sts. Work 2 rnds even (to end of color B stripe), and then change to color C.

SOLID TAIL

1. Use color C to end of tail. Work 2 rnds even. Dec rnd: K2tog, work to end. Work dec rnd every 5th rnd 15 more times—4 sts. Work 5 rnds on the last 4 sts (now a knitted cord).

2. Break working yarn and thread through a tapestry needle. Run yarn tail through remaining 4 sts and fasten securely, hiding tail inside snake body.

FINISHING

1 Stuff snake body loosely with roving, making sure there are no empty spots.

2 Thread a tapestry needle with color A and make even running sts around open end. Pull snugly to gather mouth closed and fasten securely, threading yarn tails inside body to hide.

3 Sew button eyes and ribbon tongue in place as shown with sewing needle and matching thread. Trim end of ribbon tongue into a V-shape.

TIP

Begin stuffing each snake by gently poking small amounts of roving into it with a wooden chopstick. In the photo, the head is being stuffed, but you may want to start by stuffing the narrowest part of the tail. As the body begins to fill, use your fingers to pull apart the roving that has already been stuffed in to keep it from forming lumps.

Other Ways to Choose Colors

What if the color wheel isn't your thing? That's absolutely fine! Some of the greatest color knitters never took an art class and don't give a fig for color wheels. Keep these ideas in mind to help you choose combinations you'll love.

Contrast is just as important as hue. Colors with highly contrasting values (right) will usually be more pleasing together than colors of the same value (left).

Look to nature. Flower gardens, forests, and meadows all are studies in how colors work together. Mother Nature never combines colors that "clash."

Neutrals are colors, too. Go to the zoo and look at the animals from the African plains. Brown, gold, and green have much to teach us about contrast, value, tint, tone, and shade.

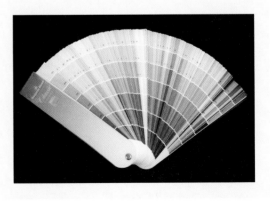

Color fans from a paint store are really useful portable color libraries. Each card shows hue, value, and saturation, all in one place. You can even write the names and amounts of yarns already in your collection on the corresponding chip in your fan. It's an instant stash inventory system.

Make proportionate combinations. If you know that bright green is only a small part of your overall composition, cover most of that skein with the other colors to get a true idea of what they will look like together.

Work within the yarn maker's palette. While you certainly are not limited to choosing yarn from only one source, keep in mind that yarn collections (from the same manufacturer) are usually created to work together. Don't be afraid to take advantage of the hard work already done for you by yarn designers.

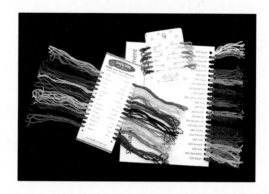

Surprise yourself. If you have some colors chosen, but don't know what else to add, ask yourself, "What color would I *never* choose to go with these?" Grab a skein of that hue and put it with those you already have. The result is often very surprising. Even if you don't like the combination, this exercise can help you think in a new direction.

TIP

Emulate your favorite ready-to-wear color combinations. Looking at fashion photos with a critical eye for the colors can be really enlightening. Remember, you don't have to love the shapes of the clothing, just pay attention to the colors.

CHAPTER 2

Color Knitting Yarns

At the same time you are choosing colors for your design, you will need to consider the material you'll use. The fiber, structure, gauge, and dye style of your yarn all contribute to the look and feel of your final product.

Fiber

After color, the fibers you knit with have the greatest impact on the finished design. Choose the fiber that offers the best drape, hand, knitting characteristics, and care requirements for your project.

CELLULOSE FIBERS

Cellulose fibers are characterized by their smoothness, crisp hand, and lack of elasticity. They are widely available, inexpensive, and easy to care for. When blended with protein or man-made fibers, cellulose yarns can exhibit the best qualities of both. Possible drawbacks: The inelastic quality of plant fibers can make yarn tails and ends difficult to hide in finished knitting. Cellulose fibers are sometimes less colorfast than protein or synthetics. The density of yarns made from these fibers can cause knitted fabrics to be heavy.

A cotton yarn sample

PROTEIN FIBERS

Widely prized for colorwork, wool and other protein fibers offer colorfastness, elasticity, and the bonus of extra warmth. Protein fibers make forgiving yarns whose ends are easy to splice and hide. Fabric knit from animal fibers is lofty and lightweight and can be fluid, fluffy, or crisp, depending on its origin and preparation. Possible drawbacks: Protein fibers require gentle care and protection from moths. Wool that has been treated for machine-washability ("superwash") may lose some of its inherent qualities, such as elasticity and the ability to felt and full (important for steeked garments).

Wool, mohair, and silk yarn samples

SYNTHETIC FIBERS

Man-made fibers are durable, inexpensive, and easy to care for. When blended with protein or plant fibers, the resulting yarns often combine the best qualities of both. For example, sock yarns spun from a combination of wool and nylon have long been loved for their mix of beauty and strength. Possible drawbacks: Purely synthetic yarns may lack the sophisticated color range of their natural counterparts and are sometimes prone to excess pilling. Pieces knit from synthetics cannot be blocked.

Nylon, acrylic, and polyester yarn samples

NON-PETROCHEMICAL SYNTHETIC FIBERS

Another group of synthetics is the cellulosic fibers. While also man-made, this variety of fiber is actually synthesized from plant matter, such as bamboo, tree bark, seaweed, corn, or even milk. These fibers are often shiny, drapey, and inelastic—qualities that mimic those of silk. As with other synthetics, combining this type of fiber with natural ones can bring out the best in both. Possible drawbacks: Although cellulosic fibers are a renewable resource, the extensive processing required to make them into yarn can make them expensive. Yarns in this group sometimes take dye unevenly. The resulting milky sheen or haze on their outer surface makes them immediately recognizable as man-made.

Bamboo and soy yarn samples

FYI While the practice of spinning fibers to form thread and yarns has been in existence for more than 10,000 years, the spinning wheel was not introduced to Europe until the late Middle Ages/early Renaissance. The primary spinning tool used to spin all the threads for clothing and fabrics before that was the hand spindle. It was used to make everything from mummy wrappings to tapestries, and even the ropes and sails for ships, for almost 9,000 years.

Yarn Structure

The way your yarn is made is as important to the finished results as what it's made from. The physical structure of a yarn has a big impact on the items you create from it. Consider the difference between a lace shawl and a cabled sweater. The yarns chosen for those projects can either enhance or detract from the unique characteristics of each. The yarn that highlights the lace's special qualities may have a very different structure from the one that best showcases the cables. Understanding the construction of yarn will help inform your color knitting choices.

One-ply yarns, commonly called *singles,* consist of only one strand of fiber.

Because singles have no other plies to balance their twist, they may tend to bias (create a slanting fabric) when knitted (a). Stitch patterns that alternate knits and purls, such as seed stitch, can counteract this problem (b).

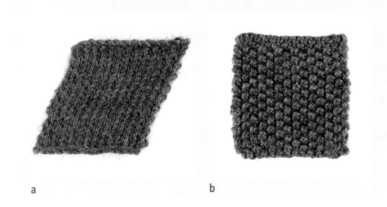

a

b

Two-ply yarns are twisted together in the reverse direction from which their individual strands are spun. Opposing the twist energy of two strands causes a yarn to be balanced. Two-ply yarns are known for the miniscule shadows created by their opposed strands. Lace and Fair Isle colorwork knitters have long prized two-ply yarns for this unique characteristic.

The tiny shadows cast by two opposing plies are part of what gives traditional Fair Isle stranded colorwork its special look. The thousands of ply shadows visually soften and blend its many intricate color changes.

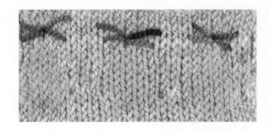

TIP

Two-ply Shetland yarn is so popular for Fair Isle stranded colorwork that it is frequently sold in smaller (25g) skeins specifically for this use. For the same price as standard 50g skeins, you can choose twice as many colors!

Three individually spun strands twisted together in the reverse direction from their spin are called a three-ply yarn. Three strands together have a rounded cross-section, and the tiny shadows of their plies are much less visible than in two-ply. Three strands make for a cohesive yarn with great strength and resistance to abrasion.

Three-ply yarn offers superior stitch definition—a huge advantage when you want to knit crisp, clear motifs. Well-defined stitches also highlight and enhance the contrast between colors.

FYI

Norwegian brides of old were expected to present their grooms, and all the men in their grooms' families, with mittens they had knitted. That's a lot of three-ply!

The more plies in a yarn, the greater its durability, and also its density. Yarn made of four plies has a "square" cross-section, making it a favorite for cables and other highly textural knitting. Four- (and more) ply yarns have traditionally been used for Aran and Gansey knitting due to this quality, combined with their high durability.

Heavily cabled knits from the Aran Islands are enhanced by the use of dense, four-ply yarn. The many plies provide lofty warmth and great durability.

Photo © Elzbieta Sekowska

Gansey knitting, with its great variation of knit-and-purl stitch patterns, is traditionally executed in smooth, dense, five-ply yarn. This lightweight yarn lends itself perfectly to the firm gauge at which Ganseys are knit.

Photo © Gordon and Margaret Reid

Yarns with a layer of fuzz outside the main core of the plies are said to have a "halo." The fabric resulting from haloed yarns has a soft, blended texture in which the difference between colors and stitches is blurred. Though sometimes delicate and pricey, yarns with halo create unmistakable effects in color knitting.

This luxury angora yarn has an unusual effect on the normally crisp lines of an argyle intarsia. Notice how the halo of the yarn literally blurs the line between colors.

Photo © Teresa Gregorio, canaryknits.blogspot.com

Sweden's Bohus knitting famously combines the halo effect of angora-blend yarns with intricate color changes and carefully placed occasional purl stitches.

Photo © Suzan Moskel

Novelty or art yarns are often comprised of mixed fibers, metallics, and even found objects. Due to their unusual nature and sometimes high cost, they are often found in small amounts in knitted colorwork. Strategic placement within the design will highlight these special yarns to best advantage.

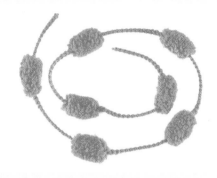

Yarns like this one can work beautifully when used with restraint. The cuff detail shown here is extravagant and luxurious compared to the smooth, commercially spun yarn used for the rest of the sweater.

TIP

Learn to spin with a hand spindle to create your own luxury art yarn. Small amounts of mohair, Lurex, and hand-dyed locks are great fun to play with, and you can easily create small amounts of handmade yarn for accents on otherwise plain knitwear.

Weight

While the number of plies decides a yarn's structure, the weight of a yarn impacts its gauge. The Craft Yarn Council of America has established standards by which yarn weights can be classified. Understanding these symbols will help you choose the proper yarn weight for your knitting. Common weights used in colorwork are shown here.

YARN WEIGHT

CYCA Yarn Weights		
Weight	**Symbol**	**Sample Yarn Strand**
SUPER FINE: Sock, Fingering	1 SUPER FINE	
FINE: Sport, Baby	2 FINE	
LIGHT: DK, Light Worsted	3 LIGHT	
MEDIUM: Worsted, Aran	4 MEDIUM	

CONSIDER BECOMING A LIGHTWEIGHT

You may notice that colorwork designs often call for lighter-weight yarns than their single-shade counterparts. The reason for this is that colorwork often requires an overlap of two or more strands, doubling the thickness of the knitted fabric. Lighter-gauge knitting is more flattering to most figures than heavy, bulky looks. Items knit at finer gauges are also usually more comfortable to wear indoors. If you have never worked at smaller gauges before, a full-scale adult sweater may seem daunting at first. Start with a small, approachable project, such as a hat, while you are getting used to working with finer needles and yarn.

Colorwork top in light-gauge yarn

In addition to what your yarn is made of and how it is constructed, remember to think about the knitted fabric it will make. For example, the fabric that looks right for a summer camisole is really different from what you'd like for a cozy afghan.

Hand refers to the way the surface of your knitted fabric feels. It's usually described in tactile terms. For example, the soft, cushiony loft of a washcloth calls for the special set of yarn characteristics found in 100% cotton yarn.

Drape is the term used to describe the way knitted fabric hangs from or hugs the body. The drape of this silk scarf is slinky and fluid.

TIP

Always take the time to acquaint yourself with your yarn by swatching. Although you also knit swatches to determine gauge, they are indispensable for discovering what sort of fabrics each yarn can become. Hand and drape are greatly influenced by the gauge at which the yarn is worked, so experiment freely until you get the fabric you like best.

Dye Techniques

Aside from the actual colors, the type of dyestuffs used and the way they are applied to yarn have as much to do with the way it looks as its fiber and structure. Modern knitters have more beautiful, high-quality yarn available for their creations than ever before. Appreciating the dyers' art will help you to choose yarns that best complement your creations.

Mill-dyed yarns are characterized by their saturated, even colors. The colors are repeatable, predictable, and marked by consistent dye lot numbers. The color palettes of some mill-dyed yarns remain unchanged for years, while other manufacturers change their offerings constantly.

Self-striping yarns are created by mills and independent dyers alike. Their special trait is the way their colors repeat in a predictable pattern. They are engineered to create repeating striped patterns when used to make socks or other narrow pieces.

FYI

The first self-striping yarns were engineered and commercially produced by large mills. Their introduction into the marketplace inspired small-scale, artisanal dyers to replicate and improve on them. Now an enormous selection of beautiful, sustainable, hand-made yarn is available from our favorite artists. In this unusual reversal, art was actually inspired by industry.

Artisan-dyed yarns are often one (or few) of a kind, unrepeatable colorways. They are characterized by their handmade, painterly qualities. Hand-painted yarns are known for their shifting, pooling, changing colors. They can be self-striping, semi-solid, or variegated.

Long-repeat color-changing yarns are made both in mills and by independent dyers. Their unique attribute is to change colors over many yards, or even entire skeins, of yarn. These slow, subtle shifts allow colors to change over an entire knitted piece rather than a predetermined stripe repeat.

You can make your own hand-dyed yarn with powdered drink mix by following these instructions:

1. Soak the undyed yarn in water to prepare it for dye.

2. In a glass container, dissolve 2 packages of unsweetened drink mix for every 50g of yarn (experiment with more or less mix to get different results).

3. Add the yarn, plus enough water to cover.

4. Microwave on high for 2 minutes, then let cool for 2 minutes.

Repeat heating and cooling until the water is almost clear or the yarn is the color you like. Let cool, then wash and hang to dry.

CHAPTER 3

Explore Stripes

A great way to begin experimenting with color in your knitting is to explore the way that stripes can change the look of a design. Nearly any knitting project can incorporate stripes, with little or no change to the pattern specifics.

Knitting of a Different Stripe

Stripes offer tremendous flexibility from a design point of view. They can be oriented either vertically or horizontally. You can knit them in any size or scale, taking advantage of their versatility to highlight or disguise different figure traits. They can also be used to set off other areas of color and texture. Stripes often add just the right amount of interest when incorporated into designs where other color knitting techniques would be too busy or distracting.

Stripe Examples

These swatches illustrate how color and texture combine to create stripes of very different sizes and moods.

NARROW STRIPES IN GARTER STITCH

The narrow stripes shown here are of a small scale. Their subtle colors, worked in garter stitch, have a soft, pebbly texture. Notice how the colors seem to blend and fade into each other.

WIDE STRIPES IN STOCKINETTE STITCH

These wide stripes are bold, bright, and energetic. Observe how their width creates a more imposing scale and how the smooth stockinette stitch enhances the contrast between colors.

SIMPLE STRIPES IN RAGLAN SHAPING

Stripes can highlight details of knitted shaping that might otherwise go unnoticed. Working this decreased square in a simple stripe repeat highlights its geometry.

IRREGULAR HORIZONTAL STRIPES

These contrasting horizontal bands of color echo the neckline, emphasizing the broadness of the shoulders.

SUBTLY GRADED STRIPES

These stripes are so subtle that they trick the eye, fading into each other to create an ombré effect.

SINGLE NARROW STRIPE

Here the impact of a single narrow stripe changes the whole spirit of the design. The simplest crewneck becomes sporty and sophisticated with the addition of a tipped edge.

Join and Carry Alternate Strands

Once you know how to add and carry different colors, making stripes in any pattern is easy. Apply these techniques to the striped projects that follow.

Join a New Color with a Weaver's Knot

1 Make a weaver's knot to join the new color as follows: With the new color, make a slipknot, and pass the old color through it. Pass the whole skein of the old color through the slipknot if you don't want to break the working strand.

2 Snug the slipknot up next to the work where you want the new color to begin (a). Gently tug the ends of the slipknot apart until the old color pops through (b).

a

b

Carry Strands Upward

1 To avoid weaving in extra yarn tails, you can change to a new color without breaking off the old one. *Carry* (strand loosely upward on the wrong side) the unused color as you knit with the new color so the old one will be close by when you are ready to switch back to it.

2 After changing colors, carry the unused strand loosely up the back of the work and twist it around the current color to anchor it to the wrong side of the piece.

TIP

The act of twisting the prior color around the current one is known as *tacking*. Tack the unused strand at the side edge of the piece every two rows when working flat, or at any interval you choose when working circularly.

Knit Stripes in Ribbing

Ribbing and other stitch patterns comprised of adjacent knit and purl stitches present a special challenge to stripe-knitters. This simple technique will keep the colors in your ribbed stripes sharp.

When changing colors in ribbing, the new color can create unsightly purl bumps that are visible on the public side of the work.

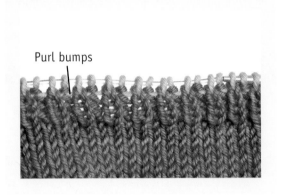

Purl bumps

Rather than maintain the ribbing stitch pattern (in this case, k1, p1) on the color-change row, knit all the stitches in that row. Change back to the stitch pattern on the following row.

Circular-knit tubes are made up of rounds rather than rows. Knitted rounds spiral one on top of another rather than stacking evenly as rows do. This characteristic of circular knitting causes "jogs" where the color changes in stripes are visible. There are several ways to make the jogs less noticeable. This section shows two of my favorites.

Here you can see what happens when changing stripe colors in circular knitting. Each time a new round begins with a new color, you can see a stair-step or "jog" in the knitting.

These stripes were knit using a technique to minimize the appearance of the jogs.

Knit One Stitch from the Prior Round

This technique for minimizing jogs is especially useful for very narrow stripes. The first stripe is complete, with one full round of the second stripe knitted.

1 Pick up last st of prev color and place it on left needle, right next to first st of new color.

2 Knit the last st and the first st together.

The jog will be visually softened and minimized. Blocking the piece at the end of knitting helps make the jog even less noticeable.

> **TIP**
>
> When planning stripes, take your construction technique into account. If you will be knitting flat, choose stripes with rows in multiples of 2. For circular knitting, stripes in any number of rows will work.

Slip One Stitch

Another way to disguise jogs is to slip one stitch. This technique makes jogs in wide stripes nearly invisible.

In this photo the first stripe is complete, with one complete round of the second stripe knitted.

When you come back to the beginning of the round, slip the first stitch to the right needle purlwise, without actually knitting it.

TIP

Yarns with both elasticity and *tooth* (surface fuzz that grips itself), such as 100% wool, make it easier to disguise jogs. Superwash wool and slippery fibers can be less forgiving.

Hexagon Hat

The paired decreases that shape the crown of this hat create miters in the stripes at six evenly spaced points. Five analogous yarn colors are repeated in the same sequence from the lower edge to the top, ending with a cord-and-tassel top decoration.

Not sure what order you want for your stripes? Try wrapping strands of different colors around a scrap of cardboard to represent the stripes, in various progressions.

Specifications

SIZE
Finished measurements: 22 (24)" circumference and 7¼ (8)" height, to fit an adult

YARN
DK-weight yarn

Shown: Simply Shetland *Lambswool & Cashmere,* 87.5% lambswool, 12.5% cashmere; 136 yd. ball

A: #555 Mallard, 1 ball

B: #273 Blueprint, 1 ball

C: #168 Vista, 1 ball

D: #004 Gaea, 1 ball

E: #453 Kingfisher, 1 ball

GAUGE
24 sts and 32 rnds = 4" in St st on larger needle

NEEDLES
Size 4 (3.5mm) 16" circular, or size needed to achieve gauge

Size 5 (3.75mm) 16" circular and DPNs, or size needed to achieve gauge

OTHER MATERIALS
Stitch marker

Tapestry needle

Pattern Stitches

Stripe Pattern: *4 rnds A, 4 rnds B, 4 rnds C, 4 rnds D,
4 rnds E; rep from * for patt.

Directions

WORK LOWER EDGE
1 With color E and smaller needle, CO 132 (144) sts.
2 PM and join for working in rnds, being careful not to twist. Work in k2, p2 rib for 8 rnds.

WORK HAT SIDES
Change to larger needle and St st. Work in stripe patt until piece measures 3½ (4)" from CO.

WORK CROWN SHAPING
1 Dec rnd 1: K9 (10), *ssk, k2tog, k18 (20); rep from * 4 more times, ssk, k2tog, k9 (10)—120 (132) sts.
2 Work 2 rnds even.

3 Cont alternating 2 knit rnds with each dec rnd as foll:

4 Dec rnd 2: K8 (9), *ssk, k2tog, k16 (18); rep from * 4 more times, ssk, k2tog, k8 (9)—108 (120) sts.

5 Dec rnd 3: K7 (8), *ssk, k2tog, k14 (16); rep from * 4 more times, ssk, k2tog, k7 (8)—96 (108) sts.

6 Dec rnd 4: K6 (7), *ssk, k2tog, k12 (14); rep from * 4 more times, ssk, k2tog, k6 (7)—84 (96) sts.

7 Dec rnd 5: K5 (6), *ssk, k2tog, k10 (12); rep from * 4 more times, ssk, k2tog, k5 (6)—72 (84) sts.

8 Dec rnd 6: K4 (5), *ssk, k2tog, k8 (10); rep from * 4 more times, ssk, k2tog, k4 (5)—60 (72) sts.

9 Dec rnd 7: K3 (4), *ssk, k2tog, k6 (8); rep from * 4 more times, ssk, k2tog, k3 (4)—48 (60) sts.

10 Dec rnd 8: K2 (3), *ssk, k2tog, k4 (6); rep from * 4 more times, ssk, k2tog, k2 (3)—36 (48) sts.

11 Dec rnd 9: K1 (2), *ssk, k2tog, k2 (4); rep from * 4 more times, ssk, k2tog, k1 (2)—24 (36) sts.

NOTE: For smaller size, omit dec rnd 10 and proceed to dec rnd 11.

12 Dec rnd 10: K1, *ssk, k2tog, k2; rep from * 4 more times, ssk, k2tog, k1—24 sts.

13 Dec rnd 11: *ssk, k2tog; rep from * 5 more times—12 sts.

14 Work 1 rnd even.

15 Next rnd: [K2tog] 6 times—6 sts.

MAKE TOP CORD

1 Using 2 DPNs and a single color, work knitted cord with last 6 sts for 2½".

2 Break yarn and thread through tapestry needle. Run tapestry needle through all sts and pull to snug. Fasten end securely.

FINISHING

1 With color E, make a 4"-long tassel and sew securely to end of cord with tapestry needle.

2 Weave in yarn tails and block.

Hexagon Hat Schematic

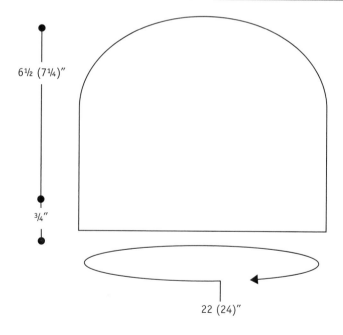

6½ (7¼)"

¾"

22 (24)"

Verticality Vest

This project relies on long-repeat self-striping yarn for its color changes. Knitting the piece from side to side causes the stripes to run vertically, for a slimming effect on the body. The texture of the purl ridges in the simple stitch pattern repeats the vertical element.

Specifications

SIZE
Finished chest measurement: 38 (40, 42, 44)"

YARN
Worsted-weight yarn

Shown: Noro *Kureyon,* 100% wool; 110 yd. ball

MC: #226 red/teal/olive/magenta, 5 (6, 7, 7) balls

CC: #260 olive/lime/salmon/black, 2 balls

GAUGE
20 sts and 28 rows = 4" in St st

NEEDLES
Size 7 (4.5mm) 24" and 16" circular needles, or size needed to achieve gauge

OTHER MATERIALS
Stitch marker

Removable markers

One 1⅛" button

One ¾" button

One ⅝" button

Tapestry needle

SPECIAL ABBREVIATIONS
MB (Make Buttonhole): K2tog, yo

Pattern Stitches

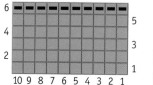

☐	k on RS, p on WS
▬	p on RS, k on WS

Directions

WORK LEFT FRONT

❶ With MC, CO 78 (80, 82, 84) sts.

❷ Work even in charted patt until piece measures 3½ (4, 4½, 5)" from CO, ending with a RS row.

SHAPE LEFT FRONT NECKLINE

❶ CO 24 sts at beg of next WS row. 102 (104, 106, 108) sts.

❷ Work even in patt until piece measures 6½ (7, 7½, 8)" from CO, ending with a RS row.

SHAPE LEFT ARMHOLE

❶ Next row (WS): BO 40 sts, work to end of row. BO 3 sts at beg of next 5 WS rows—47 (49, 51, 53) sts.

❷ Work even in patt until piece measures 9¾ (10¾, 11¾, 12¾)" from CO, ending with a RS row.

❸ CO 3 sts at beg of next 5 WS rows. CO 40 sts at beg of foll WS row—102 (104, 106, 108) sts.

❹ Work even in patt until piece measures 14 (15, 16, 17)" from CO, ending with a RS row.

SHAPE BACK NECKLINE

① BO 5 sts at beg of next WS row. BO 3 sts at beg of foll WS row. BO 1 st at beg of next 3 WS rows— 91 (93, 95, 97) sts.

② Work even in patt until piece measures 23 (24, 25, 26)" from CO, ending with a RS row.

③ Inc 1 st at beg of next 3 WS rows. CO 3 sts at beg of foll WS row. CO 5 sts at beg of next WS row—102 (104, 106, 108) sts.

④ Work even in patt until piece measures 27 (28, 29, 30)" from CO, ending with a RS row.

SHAPE RIGHT ARMHOLE

① BO 40 sts at beg of next WS row. BO 3 sts at beg of foll 5 WS rows—47 (49, 51, 53) sts.

② Work even in patt until piece measures 30¼ (31¾, 33¼, 34¾)" from CO, ending with a RS row.

③ CO 3 sts at beg of next 5 WS rows. CO 40 sts at beg of foll WS row—102 (104, 106, 108) sts.

④ Work even in patt until piece measures 34½ (36, 37½, 39)" from CO, ending with a RS row.

SHAPE RIGHT FRONT NECKLINE

① BO 24 sts at beg of next WS row—78 (80, 82, 84) sts.

② Work even in patt until piece measures 38 (40, 42, 44)" from CO. BO.

FINISHING

Work bottom edging

Working from RS, with CC, pick up and knit 204 (214, 226, 236) sts along lower edge of vest. Work in k1, p1 rib for 1". BO. Block vest.

Sew shoulder seams with MC and a tapestry needle.

Stripe Yoke Turtleneck Schematic

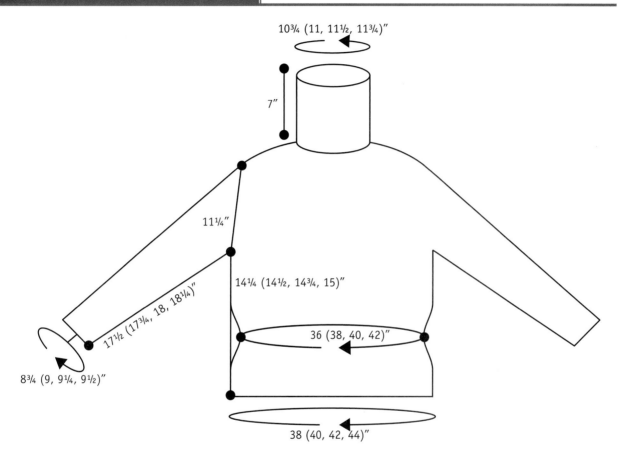

10¾ (11, 11½, 11¾)"

7"

11¼"

17½ (17¾, 18, 18¼)"

14¼ (14½, 14¾, 15)"

36 (38, 40, 42)"

8¾ (9, 9¼, 9½)"

38 (40, 42, 44)"

UNEVEN STRIPES

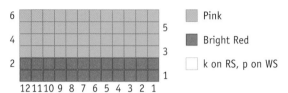

Pink

Bright Red

k on RS, p on WS

ALTERNATING STOCKINETTE AND REVERSE STOCKINETTE STITCH STRIPES
(5 rows St st, 3 rows rev St st)

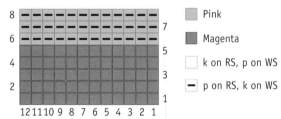

Pink

Magenta

k on RS, p on WS

— p on RS, k on WS

TWO-ROW GARTER STRIPES

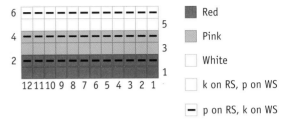

■	Red	
■	Pink	
□	White	
□	k on RS, p on WS	
—	p on RS, k on WS	

REVERSE-STOCKINETTE STRIPES WITH KNIT RIDGES

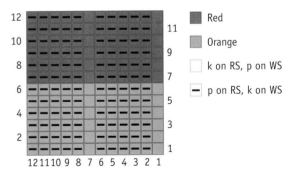

■	Red	
■	Orange	
□	k on RS, p on WS	
—	p on RS, k on WS	

53

RANDOM STRIPES IN SIX COLORS

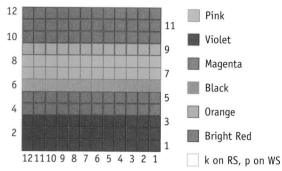

- Pink
- Violet
- Magenta
- Black
- Orange
- Bright Red
- k on RS, p on WS

1-ROW STOCKINETTE STRIPES WITH BOBBLES

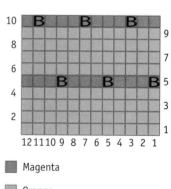

Magenta

Orange

k on RS, o on WS

B Make Bobble (RS): k into f, b, f, b of same st (make 4 from 1). *Sl 4 sts back to left needle, k4. Rep from *2 more times. Pass 2nd, 3rd, and 4th sts over 1st.
Make Bobble (WS): k into f, b, f, b of same st (make 4 from 1). *Sl 4 sts back to left needle, p4. Rep from *2 more times. Pass 2nd, 3rd, and 4th sts over 1st.

STRIPED BASKETWEAVE

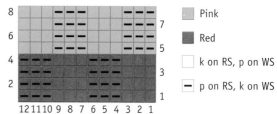

- ▢ Pink
- ▇ Red
- ▢ k on RS, p on WS
- ▬ p on RS, k on WS

FIBONACCI SEQUENCE STRIPES

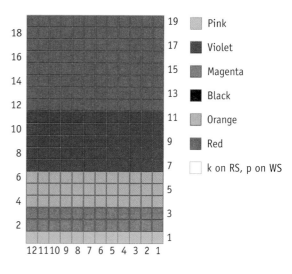

- ▢ Pink
- ▇ Violet
- ▇ Magenta
- ▇ Black
- ▢ Orange
- ▇ Red
- ▢ k on RS, p on WS

ALTERNATING VERTICAL STRIPES

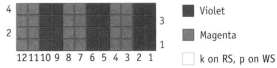

- ■ Violet
- ■ Magenta
- □ k on RS, p on WS

CORRUGATED RIBBING

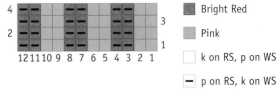

- ■ Bright Red
- ■ Pink
- □ k on RS, p on WS
- — p on RS, k on WS

ZIGZAG STRIPES

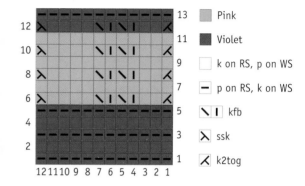

Symbol	Meaning
	Pink
	Violet
	k on RS, p on WS
−	p on RS, k on WS
\ I	kfb
⅄	ssk
⅃	k2tog

FEATHER AND FAN

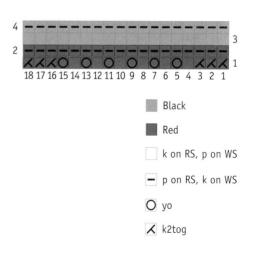

Symbol	Meaning
	Black
	Red
	k on RS, p on WS
−	p on RS, k on WS
O	yo
⅃	k2tog

CHAPTER 4

Discover Slip-Stitch Patterns

Slip-stitch patterns are a logical next step after stripes in your color knitting journey. While still basically knitting stripes, using one strand of yarn at a time, you create color patterns by slipping stitches at predetermined intervals. Simple, yet stunning!

One Strand at a Time

For any knitter new to color knitting, the prospect of handling two or more strands of yarn at a time may seem daunting. Enter the magic of slipped stitches: You only one use strand at a time, while creating beautiful, intricate-looking patterns.

Slip-Stitch Examples

GEOMETRIC PATTERNS

Slip-stitch patterns lend themselves easily to patterns with straight lines and sharp corners. Patterns like this one are sometimes referred to as *mosaic knitting,* a term coined by Barbara Walker. Walker's extensive explorations of the technique provide excellent further reading.

ROUNDED PATTERNS

Slipped stitches can also make patterns with curved-looking or "bent" edges. It's hard to believe that these are basically just stripes.

These samples show how slipped stitches can create effects that are striking or subtle, sophisticated or whimsical. The dye technique of the yarn you select has great impact on your project's finished look with slip-stitch patterns.

HAND-PAINTED YARNS

The irregular, painterly quality of hand-dyed yarn lends itself beautifully to slip-stitch patterns, adding depth and dimension to the knitted fabric.

VARIEGATED YARNS

Slipped stitches have the unique ability to highlight different areas of variegated yarn strands. Notice how the slipped stitches cause certain colors to pop out visually.

MILL-DYED YARNS

The saturated even tones of commercially dyed yarns provide a reliable and predictable outcome in slip-stitch patterns. These yarns are the best to use when you want full control over where and how each color appears.

COLOR-CHANGING YARNS

Relinquish control over the color placement by choosing a long-repeat self-striping yarn, and the results will surprise and delight you. The subtle shifts in color in these yarns are highlighted beautifully in slip-stitch patterns.

Understand the Slipped Stitch

Slip-stitch patterns are simple to work because they repeat at predetermined intervals, and because you knit with only a single strand of yarn at any given time.

Learn the Slipping Technique

In the basic slip-stitch pattern, the stitch is passed from the left needle to the right needle without being knitted. This causes different colors from prior rows to be pulled up into the current row.

wyif

You create different effects by holding the working strand either in front of the work (wyif = with yarn in front, as above) or behind it (wyib = with yarn in back, as shown here).

wyib

Slip Purlwise or Knitwise

In addition to where you hold the working yarn, slip-stitch patterns also specify the way in which you move each slipped stitch from one needle to the other.

To slip *purlwise,* insert the right needle into the stitch as if to purl, then move it to the right needle.

purlwise

To slip *knitwise,* insert the right needle into the stitch as if to knit, then move it to the right needle.

knitwise

TIP

A note about slip-stitch fabric: Slipping stitches creates a fabric that is more compressed vertically. Make swatches to determine the gauge that creates the best fabric: neither too dense nor too loose.

Flame-Stitch Chart

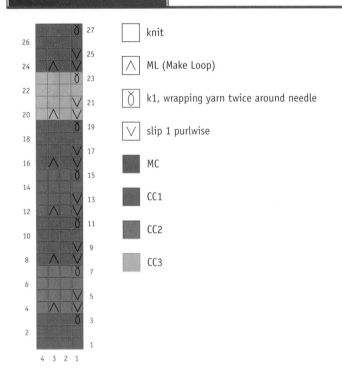

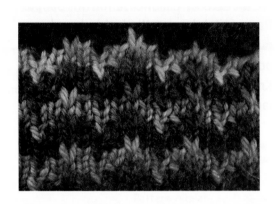

Legend:

- ☐ knit
- ∧ ML (Make Loop)
- ठ k1, wrapping yarn twice around needle
- ∨ slip 1 purlwise
- ■ MC
- ■ CC1
- ■ CC2
- ■ CC3

ML: Insert right needle into next st, 2 rows below, and pull up a loop of yarn. Knit next st and pass loop over st just knit.

Directions for the Beret

WORK LOWER EDGE

1 With CC1 and smaller DPNs, work 5-st knitted cord for 35". Run yarn tail through live sts to secure.

2 Measure 7½ (7)" from end of cord and place removable marker. With MC and larger circular needle, beginning at M, pick up and knit 140 (148) sts, ending 7½ (7)" from end of cord. PM and join for working in rnds.

WORK BAND

Work Rows 1–27 of flame-stitch chart once.

WORK BERET BODY

1 With MC, *k1, kfb. Rep from * to end of rnd—210
(222) sts.

2 Work even until piece measures 5½ (6)" from bottom
of knitted cord.

WORK CROWN SHAPING

1 Place 6 markers so that there are 35
(37) sts between each pair.

2 Dec 12 sts every other rnd as foll: *Ssk,
work to 2 sts before M, k2tog. Rep from
* to end of rnd. Rep dec rnd every other
rnd 15 (16) more times—18 sts.

3 Next rnd: *Ssk, k1. Rep from * to end of
rnd—12 sts. Next rnd: Knit. Next rnd:
[ssk] 6 times—6 sts. Break yarn and
thread through tapestry needle. Run
yarn tail through last 6 sts, fastening
securely on WS.

FINISHING

Weave in yarn tails and block, stretching
gently over an 11" dinner plate to shape.
Tie cord ends in a bow as shown.

Directions for the Mittens

WORK LOWER EDGE

1. With CC1 and smaller DPNs, work 5-st knitted cord for 20". Run yarn tail through live sts to secure.

2. Measure 7½ (7)" from end of cord and place removable marker. With MC and larger DPN, beg at M, pick up and knit 52 (56) sts, ending 7½ (7)" from end of cord. PM and join for working in rnds.

WORK CUFF

Work rows 1–27 of flame-stitch chart once.

CREATE THUMB GUSSET

1. Next rnd: With MC, knit to end of rnd, then inc 1 st—53 (57) sts.

2. Next rnd: K26 (28), PM, M1L, k1, M1R, PM, knit to end of rnd—55 (59) sts. Knit 1 rnd. Next rnd: K26 (28), sl M, M1L, knit to M, M1R, sl M, work to end of rnd—2 sts inc'd. Knit 2 rnds.

3. Rep incs every 3rd rnd 7 more times (19 sts between M).

4. Next rnd: Knit to M, remove M, place next 19 sts on waste yarn for gusset (do not remove M), knit to end of rnd—52 (56) sts.

5. Next rnd: Knit to M, sl M, inc 1 st over gap that forms over thumb gusset, knit to end of rnd—53 (57) sts.

WORK HAND

Work even until piece measures 7¼ (7½)" from bottom of knitted cord. Dec 1 st at end of next rnd—52 (56) sts.

DECREASE MITTEN TOP

Rnd 1: K1, ssk, knit to 3 sts before M, k2tog, k1, sl M, k1, ssk, knit to last 3 sts, k2tog, k1.

Rnd 2: Knit.

Rep rnds 1 and 2 6 (7) more times—24 sts. Graft rem sts with Kitchener st.

WORK THUMB

Place held sts onto larger DPN and CO 1 st over gap formed by gusset—20 sts. Work even until thumb measures 1¾ (2)" from pickup rnd.

Next rnd: [K2tog] 10 times—10 sts. Knit 1 rnd.

Next rnd: [K2tog] 5 times—5 sts.

Break yarn and thread through rem 5 sts, gathering snugly. Fasten securely on WS.

FINISHING

Weave in yarn tails on WS, darning gap at base of thumb closed. Tie ends of knitted cord in a bow as shown.

Make a second mitten to match.

Flambé Beret and Mitten Schematic

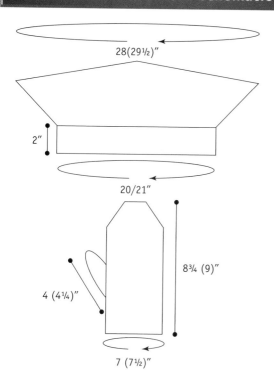

28(29½)"

2"

20/21"

8¾ (9)"

4 (4¼)"

7 (7½)"

Scarf Noir

Worked at a very fine gauge, this scarf takes advantage of the yarn's softness, in addition to highlighting its magical color changes. As you work, watch the colors shift and change throughout both skeins. The geometric tessellations of this slip-stitch pattern trick the eye, while the drape of the fabric delights the touch.

Specifications

SIZE
Finished measurements: 9" wide × 34½" long

YARN
Fingering-weight yarn

Shown: Crystal Palace Yarns *Sausalito,* 80% superwash merino/20% nylon, 198 yd.

MC: #8306 Firebird (reds), 2 balls

CC: #8307 French Roast (grays), 2 balls

GAUGE
42 sts and 73 rows = 4" in patt st

NEEDLES
Size 1 (2.25mm) needles, or size needed to achieve gauge

NOTIONS
Tapestry needle

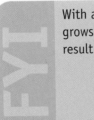

FYI

With about 18 rows to the inch, this scarf grows very slowly as you work. The finished result is worthy of your patience.

Work Left Front Band

1 With smaller needles and MC, pick up and knit 74 (82, 88) sts along edge of left front, working from RS and beg at upper edge.

2 Work in seed st until edging measures ¾" from beg. BO.

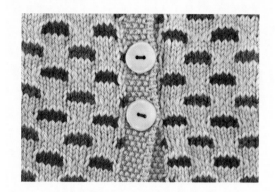

Work Right Front Band

1 With smaller needles and MC, pick up and knit 74 (82, 88) sts along right front, working from RS and beg at lower edge. Work in seed st for 3 rows, ending with a WS row.

2 Next row (RS): Work to last 32 sts. *Work 6 sts, k2tog, double yo, ssk. Rep from * twice more, work last 2 sts.

3 Next row (WS): Work in seed st, knitting into front & back of each double yo from prev row. Work 2 more rows in seed st. BO.

4 Steam bands lightly to block.

5 Sew buttons to left band under buttonholes.

Baby Bubbles Cardigan Schematic

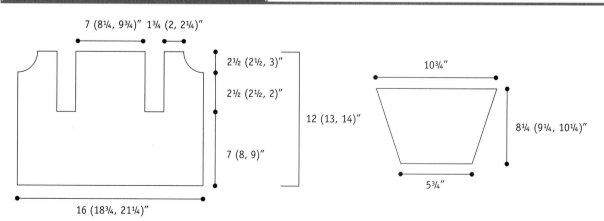

BRICKS

	Variegated Orange
	Light Orange
	k on RS, p on WS
—	p on RS, k on WS
⋁	Sl 1 pwise wyib on RS, SL 1 pwise wyif on WS

CHAIN LINKS

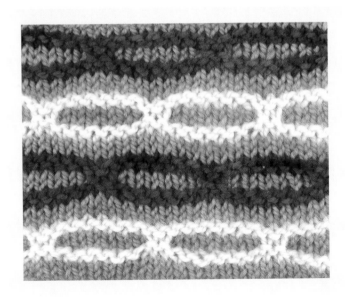

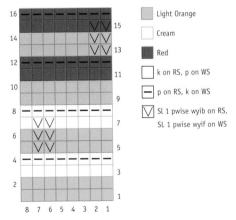

	Light Orange
	Cream
	Red
	k on RS, p on WS
—	p on RS, k on WS
⋁	Sl 1 pwise wyib on RS, SL 1 pwise wyif on WS

CHECKS

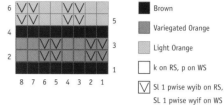

- Brown
- Variegated Orange
- Light Orange
- ☐ k on RS, p on WS
- ☑ Sl 1 pwise wyib on RS, SL 1 pwise wyif on WS

CHECKS AND RIDGES

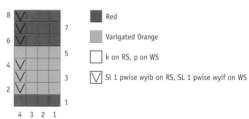

- Red
- Varigated Orange
- ☐ k on RS, p on WS
- ☑ Sl 1 pwise wyib on RS, SL 1 pwise wyif on WS

77

DIPPED STITCH

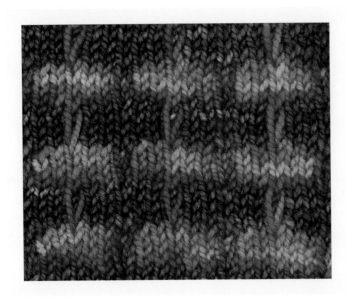

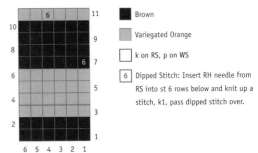

■ Brown

▨ Variegated Orange

□ k on RS, p on WS

6 Dipped Stitch: Insert RH needle from RS into st 6 rows below and knit up a stitch, k1, pass dipped stitch over.

HEXAGON

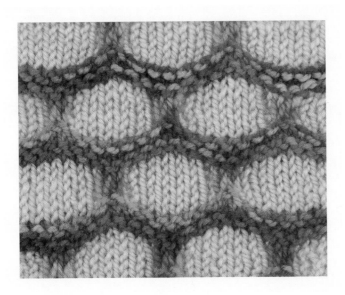

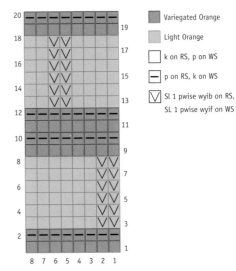

▨ Variegated Orange

▨ Light Orange

□ k on RS, p on WS

— p on RS, k on WS

Ⅴ Sl 1 pwise wyib on RS, SL 1 pwise wyif on WS

LINKAGE

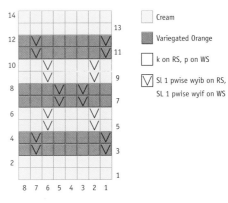

Cream

Variegated Orange

k on RS, p on WS

V Sl 1 pwise wyib on RS,
SL 1 pwise wyif on WS

SADDLE BLANKET

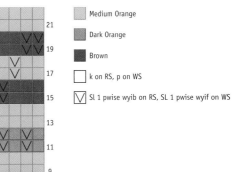

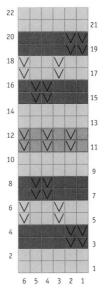

Medium Orange

Dark Orange

Brown

k on RS, p on WS

V Sl 1 pwise wyib on RS, SL 1 pwise wyif on WS

SHADOW BOX

- Apircot
- Red
- Light Orange
- k on RS, p on WS
- ⋁ Sl 1 pwise wyib on RS, SL 1 pwise wyif on WS
- ℧ k on WS, wrapping yarn twice
- ✳ Sl 1 pwise wyif, letting extra wrap fall off needle

SLIPPED VERTICAL RIB

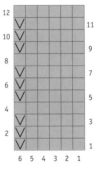

- k on RS, p on WS
- ⋁ Sl 1 pwise wyib on RS, SL 1 pwise wyif on WS

SPROUTS

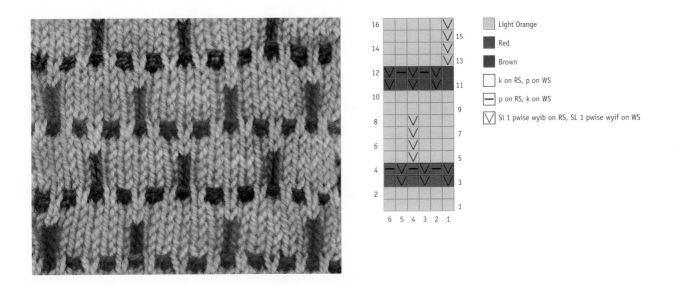

	16							
16					V			15
14						V		
					V			13
12	V	—	V	V				
	V		V	V			11
10								
								9
8			V					
			V					7
6			V					
			V					5
4		—	V	V	—	V		
			V	V	V			3
2								
								1
	6	5	4	3	2	1	

Light Orange

Red

Brown

k on RS, p on WS

— p on RS, k on WS

V Sl 1 pwise wyib on RS, Sl 1 pwise wyif on WS

WINDOWPANES

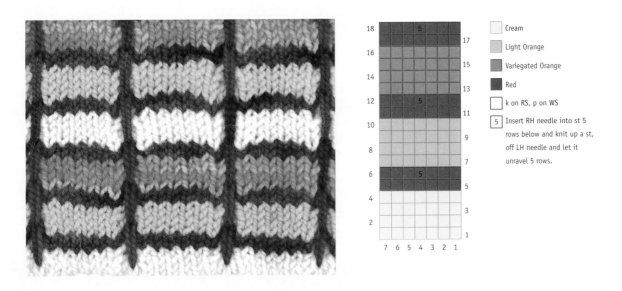

Cream

Light Orange

Variegated Orange

Red

k on RS, p on WS

5 Insert RH needle into st 5 rows below and knit up a st, off LH needle and let it unravel 5 rows.

CHAPTER 5

Discover Stranded Colorwork

Learn how two strands are better than one as you explore the world of stranded colorwork knitting. Thought to have originated in colder climates, a version of stranded knitting is featured in nearly every culture where knitting is done. Warmer and more durable than single-strand knitting, stranded colorwork is best known for its beautiful and intricate-looking knitted pictures, or *motifs*.

Stranded Colorwork Revealed

The secret behind the beautiful designs in stranded colorwork is in the stranding. Using two strands of yarn at a time enables the knitter to create designs, or *motifs,* in the knitted fabric. It also creates fabrics that are warmer and more durable than single-color knitting. The vast majority of stranded colorwork uses only two colors in each row, and only one strand is used at a time.

FAIR ISLE

Made famous by knitwear from Fair Isle, one of the islands of Scotland, the Fair Isle technique is one form of stranded colorwork. Fair Isle is typified by its use of symmetrical geometric motifs, two-ply Shetland yarn, and muted, sophisticated colors.

SCANDINAVIAN

Stranded colorwork originating in Scandinavia (Norway, Sweden, Denmark, and Finland) is very different from Fair Isle, though the knitting techniques are similar. Scandinavian colorwork is distinctive in its large, often asymmetrical motifs, three-ply yarn construction, and bright, clear colors.

Although the finished result may look intricate, there are really only two things you need to be aware of to get started making gorgeous stranded colorwork.

STRAND ORIENTATION

The first thing to understand about stranding is the orientation of one strand to the other. Decide which strand will be "A" and which will be "B." You will knit with only one strand at a time, while the other waits for its turn. When you change from using one color to another, keep their orientation consistent:

"A" is the background, or receding, color, and that strand should always cross *below* the other.

"B" is the foreground, or outstanding, color, and that strand should always cross *above* the other.

FLOAT TENSION

The second key to stranded colorwork is making the strands of the unused color loose enough to keep the work from puckering. When changing colors, stretch apart the last stitches made in the prior color, and then loosely lay the new color across them on the wrong side. This strand on the back of the work is called a *float*. Knit with the new color, releasing the tension on the previous stitches. A properly tensioned float will relax into a "swag" or "smile" on the wrong side.

Stranding Myths

H ere are some common misconceptions about stranded colorwork.

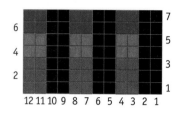

You must carry strands in the left hand, the right hand, or both hands.

This myth probably comes from the fact that in other countries, knitters don't always throw with the right hand or pick with the left hand. The fact is, any way you like to knit will yield beautiful results. Whichever hand you use to wrap the yarn is the one you should use for stranding. To begin, just drop the unused color. When you are ready to change colors, let go of the previous strand and retrieve the other one. Though it feels awkward at first, your body will soon find the way it likes to hold the strands, and your speed will increase.

You have to twist the strands around one another to avoid holes in your work.

This statement is true only if you are working in intarsia (described in Chapter 6), which is a completely different form of knitting. In stranded colorwork, twisting the strands is rarely necessary. In fact, doing so can make for twisted tangles and slanting stitches.

You can knit only a particular number of stitches at a time before you are required to change colors.

This myth originates from the tradition of Fair Isle colorwork, whose motifs are usually based on repeats of 3, 4, 5, or 7 stitches. If you are working a Fair Isle motif, just follow the chart without worrying about the number of stitches. Follow the same advice for Scandinavian-style motifs.

Songbirds Charts

SONGBIRDS YOKE CHART

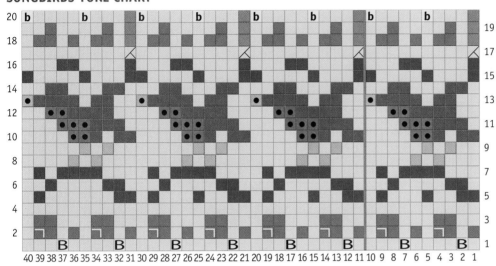

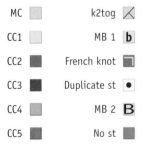

MC		k2tog	
CC1		MB 1	**b**
CC2		French knot	
CC3		Duplicate st	●
CC4		MB 2	**B**
CC5		No st	
CC6			

SLEEVE CHART

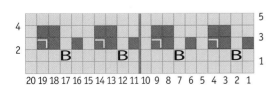

Directions

WORK LOWER EDGE

1 With larger 24" circular needle and CC3, CO 230 (240, 250, 270) sts.

2 PM and join for working in rnds, being careful not to twist sts. Knit 2 rnds in k1, p1 rib. Change to MC and knit 1 rnd. Work 3 rnds in k1, p1 rib.

WORK BODY

1 Work in St st until piece measures 3½ (4, 4½, 5)" from beg.

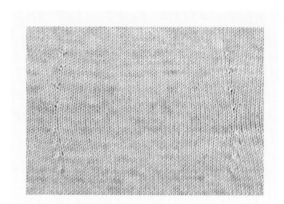

2 PM for waist shaping darts (shown at right) as follows: K38 (40, 41, 45), PM, k39 (40, 43, 45), PM, k76 (80, 82, 90), PM, k39 (40, 43, 45), PM, knit to end of rnd.

3 Next rnd: Work dec as foll: *Knit to last 2 sts before M, ssk, slip M. Knit to M, slip M, k2tog. Knit to last 2 sts before M, ssk, slip M. Knit to M, slip M, k2tog. Knit to end of rnd. Rep from * every 4th rnd, 3 more times—214 (224, 234, 254) sts.

4 Work even for 8 rnds.

5 Next rnd: Work inc as follows: *Knit to M, M1R, slip M. Knit to M, slip M, M1L. Knit to M, M1R, slip M. Knit to M, slip M, M1L. Knit to end of rnd. Rep from * every 6th rnd 3 more times—230 (240, 250, 270) sts.

6 Work even until piece measures 14½ (15, 15½, 16)" from beg. Place 18 (18, 20, 22) sts at each side of body on holders for underarms—194 (204, 210, 226) sts.

MAKE SLEEVES

1 With smaller DPNs and CC3, CO 70 (70, 80, 80) sts. Work 2 rnds in k1, p1 rib. Change to MC and knit 1 rnd. Work 3 rnds in k1, p1 rib.

2 Change to larger DPNs and work rows 1–5 of sleeve chart.

3 Next rnd—work lower sleeve gathers: K15, knit into
f & b of next 40 (40, 50, 50) sts, k15—110 (110,
130, 130) sts.

4 Work even until piece measures 1½ (2, 2½, 3)"
from beg. Place 18 (18, 20, 22) underarm sts on
holders—92 (92, 110, 110) sts.

5 Make a second sleeve to match.

JOIN SLEEVES TO BODY

1 Beg with left sleeve, rejoin working yarn and work
from 1st st adjoining holder around to last using
larger 24" circular needle.

2 Continue working all sts of body front onto same needle.

3 When you reach 2nd set of held underarm sts on body, add 2nd sleeve by working all sts from one side of
held sleeve sts to the other.

4 Work rem body sts onto same needle, PM at end of row—378 (388, 430, 442) sts.

5 Work even until body measures 17½ (18, 18½, 19)" from beg.

WORK FIRST SET OF YOKE DECREASES

1 Next rnd: PM on either side of 76 (80, 86, 88) center
sleeve sts—113 (114, 129, 133) body sts between
markers.

2 K76 (80, 86, 88) sleeve sts. *K3, k2tog. Rep from *
21 (21, 24, 25) more times to last 3 (4, 4, 3) sts
before M, k3 (4, 4, 3), slip M. K76 (80, 86, 88) sts.
*K3, k2tog. Rep from * 21 (21, 24, 25) more times
to last 3 (4, 0, 3) sts before M, k3 (4, 4, 3), slip M.
91 (92, 104, 107) body sts between markers.

NOTE: This set of decreases is worked on the body
stitches only.

3 Work even until piece measures 18½ (19, 19½, 20)" from beg.

WORK SECOND SET OF YOKE DECREASES AND UPPER SLEEVE GATHERS

1 First sleeve: Slip M, k2tog 38 (40, 43, 44) times—38 (40, 43, 44) sleeve sts.

2 Front: Slip M, *k2, k2tog. Rep from * to last 7 (4, 8, 3) sts. k2tog 3 (0, 3, 0) times K1 (4, 2, 3)—67 (70, 77, 81) front body sts.

3 Second sleeve: Work same as first sleeve—38 (40, 43, 44) sleeve sts.

4 Back: Work same as Front—67 (70, 77, 81) back body sts.

5 Total amount of yoke sts—210 (220, 240, 250) sts.

WORK BACK-NECK SHAPING (SHORT ROWS)

1 Turn work. Sl1, p39 (41, 43, 45).

Turn work. Sl1, k11 (13, 15, 17).

Turn work. Sl1, p25 (27, 29, 31).

Turn work. Sl1, k39 (41, 43, 45).

Turn work. Sl1, p53 (55, 57, 59).

Turn work. Sl1, knit to beg of rnd.

2 Neatening rnd: Knit. As you come to each previously slipped st, pick up the st in the row beneath it and place it back on left needle. Knit it and the slipped st together.

WORK YOKE

1 Work rows 1–31 of Songbirds Chart, incorporating decreases as indicated.

NOTE: Some rows of this chart call for 3 strands of yarn to be used in the same row. If you prefer, work the 3rd color in MC, then work duplicate sts as indicated on chart with the 3rd color after knitting is complete.

2 Change to smaller 16" circular needle and work 3 rnds in k1, p1 rib. Change to CC3 and knit 1 rnd. Work 1 rnd in k1, p1 rib. BO in patt.

FINISHING

❶ Work French knots and duplicate sts with tapestry needle and yarn colors as indicated on chart.

❷ Graft underarm sts using Kitchener st.

❸ Weave in ends and steam lightly to block.

2

Songbirds Schematic

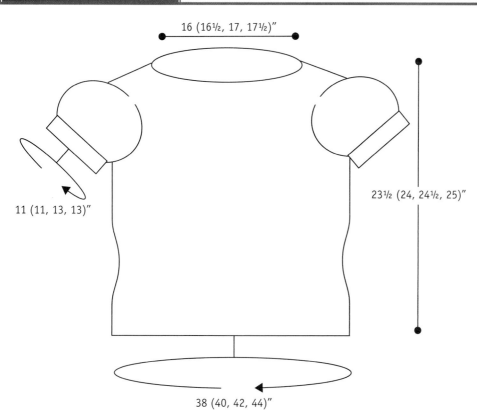

16 (16½, 17, 17½)"

23½ (24, 24½, 25)"

11 (11, 13, 13)"

38 (40, 42, 44)"

Finniquoy Waistcoat

Named for a shady ravine on Fair Isle, this vest is a classic example of traditional Fair Isle knitting. Seven colors of two-ply wool create a cohesive knitted fabric, while crocheted steeks provide a simple and elegant steek finishing technique.

NOTE: Finniquoy is designed in a modern, short length, which ends at the natural waist. For a more traditional look, increase the body length below the armholes by approximately 3–4".

Specifications

SIZE
Finished chest measurement: 36 (38, 40, 42)"

YARN
2-ply Sportweight yarn

Shown: Black Water Abbey, 100% wool, 350 yd., 4 oz.

MC: Black, 1 (2, 2, 2) skeins

CC1: Cinnamon (brown), 1 skein [2 (3, 3, 4) oz.]

CC2: Haw (red), 1 skein [1 (2, 2, 2) oz.]

CC3: Pippin (green), 1 skein [1 (2, 2, 2) oz.]

CC4: Silver (light gray), 1 skein [1 (1, 2, 2) oz.]

CC5: Moss (blue-green), 1 skein [1 (1, 2, 2) oz.]

CC6: Jacob (dark gray), 1 skein [1 (1, 1, 1) oz.]

CC7: Autumn (gold), 1 skein [1 (1, 1, 1) oz.]

GAUGE
28 sts and 36 rows = 4" in St st with larger needles

NEEDLES
Size 3 (3.25mm) 24" and 16" circular

Size 4 (3.5mm) 24" circular, or size needed to achieve gauge

NOTIONS
6 stitch markers

Tapestry needle

Crochet hook

Finniquoy Waistcoat Charts

LOWER EDGE CHART

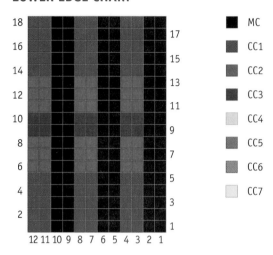

■	MC
■	CC1
■	CC2
■	CC3
☐	CC4
■	CC5
■	CC6
☐	CC7

UPPER EDGE CHART

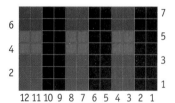

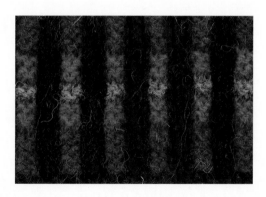

BODY CHART

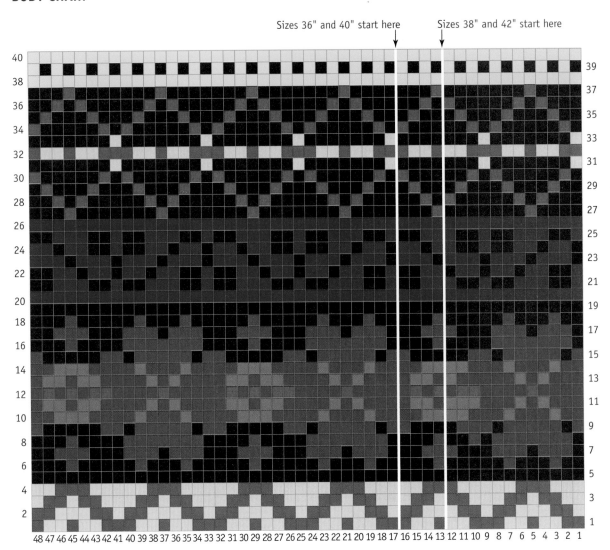

Sizes 36" and 40" start here

Sizes 38" and 42" start here

CORRUGATED RIB PATTERN

K2 in MC, p2 in CC

CHART A

MC

CC

k all sts

Pattern Repeat

← Size 38" starts here

← Size 40" starts here

← Size 42" starts here

← Size 44" starts here

103

CHART B

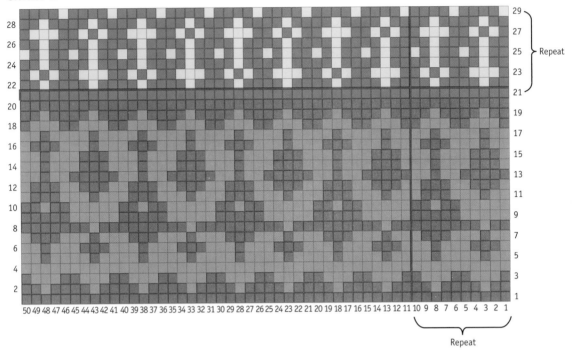

CHART C

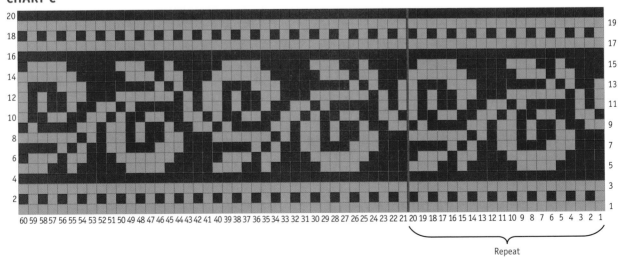

Directions

WORK KNITTED HEM

1 With smaller 24" circular needle and CC, CO 270 (280, 300, 310) sts.

2 Work back and forth in St st, (p on WS, k on RS) for 7 rows. Purl 1 row on RS for turning ridge. Change to larger 24" circular needle and work in St st for 7 rows, knitting in hem on Row 7, if desired.

WORK BODY

1 CO 6 steek sts for each armhole and 6 sts for center front and join for working in rnds, being careful not to twist sts. PM at either side of center front steek.

NOTE: Center front steek sts are excluded from stitch counts.

2 Join MC and work rows 1–53 of Chart A.

3 Work rows 1–29 of Chart B. Rep rows 21–29 until piece measures approximately 20 (20, 21, 21)" from beg. Work rows 1–20 of Chart C.

NOTE: Sizes 36 and 44 end with a half repeat of Chart C.

4 Divide live sts by moving from needle to waste yarn as follows: BO 3 sts of center front steek—23 (23, 24, 26) sts for right front neckline, 43 (45, 49, 50) sts for right front shoulder. BO 6 sts for armhole steek—43 (45, 49, 50) sts for right back shoulder, 46 (48, 50, 52) sts for back neckline, 43 (45, 49, 50) sts for left back shoulder. BO 6 sts for armhole steek—43 (45, 49, 50) sts for left front shoulder, 23 (23, 24, 26) sts for left front neckline. BO 3 sts of center front steek.

WORK SLEEVES (TWO AT A TIME)

1 Make cuff hems: With smaller circular needle and CC, CO 64 (64, 74, 74) sts and work back and forth in St st for 7 rows. Purl 1 row on RS for turning ridge. Change to larger circular needle and St st for 7 rows, knitting in hem on Row 7, if desired. Place cuff on spare needle or waste yarn. Make 2nd cuff to match.

2 Next row (RS): Knit across 64 (64, 74, 74) sts of 1st cuff, PM, CO 6 steek sts, PM, knit across 64 (64, 74, 74) sts of 2nd cuff, PM, CO 6 steek sts, PM. Join for working in rnds, being careful not to twist.

3 Work rows 1–8 of Chart A. Work rows 1–20 of Chart C. Work rows 1–29 of Chart B. *At the same time,* work inc at each side of each sleeve every 6th rnd, 23 times—110 (110, 120, 120) sts for each sleeve. Work even until sleeves measure 17 (17, 18, 18)" from turning ridge. Work rows 1–20 of Chart C. (**NOTE:** Sizes 38 and 40 end with a half repeat of Chart C.) BO steek sts and place live sleeve sts on waste yarn holders.

SECURE AND CUT STEEKS

1 Machine-stitch center front steek, following directions in Chapter 10. Cut steek and block body.

2 Machine-stitch sleeve steeks, following directions in Chapter 10. Cut sleeve steeks to separate and block sleeves.

3 Sew sleeves with yarn and tapestry needle, working from RS. Cover steek edges on WS of sleeve with ribbon or bias binding by sewing in place by hand, invisibly from WS.

4 Measure sleeve from top fold to seam. Measure same distance from top of sweater body at sleeve location. Mark with waste yarn as shown in directions in Chapter 10. Machine-stitch armhole steeks and cut.

5 Measure and mark neckline curve to a depth of 3", following directions in Chapter 10. Cut neckline curve.

GARLAND

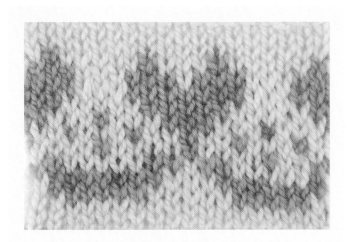

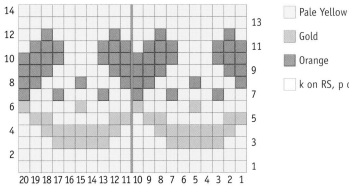

Pale Yellow

Gold

Orange

k on RS, p on WS

GINGER CAT

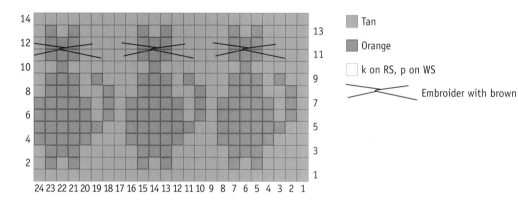

Tan

Orange

k on RS, p on WS

Embroider with brown

HEART

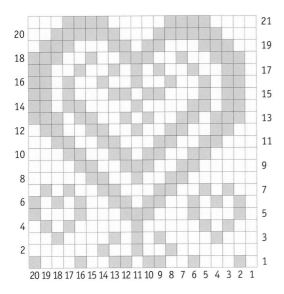

□ Cream

▨ Gold

□ k on RS, p on WS

POMEGRANATE

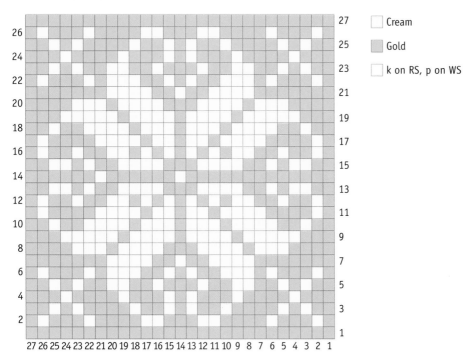

☐ Cream

▨ Gold

☐ k on RS, p on WS

REINDEER

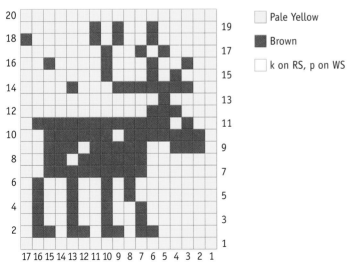

☐ Pale Yellow

■ Brown

☐ k on RS, p on WS

ROSE

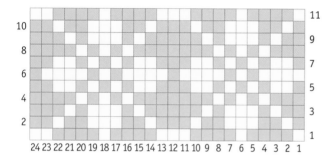

☐ Cream

▨ Gold

☐ k on RS, p on WS

SELBUROSE

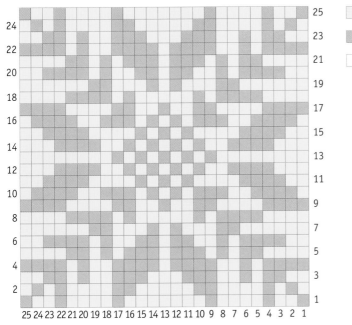

☐ Pale Yellow

☐ Gold

☐ k on RS, p on WS

STRAWBERRIES

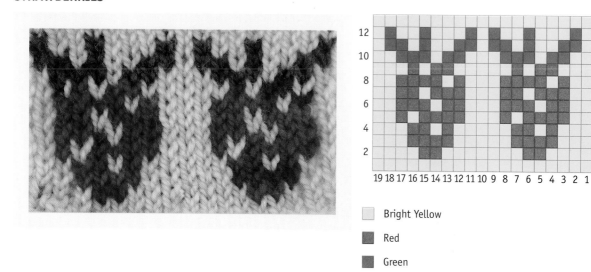

Bright Yellow

Red

Green

k on RS, p on WS

SUCCOTASH

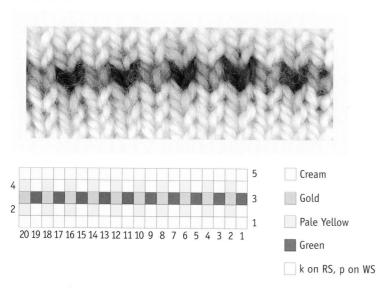

Cream

Gold

Pale Yellow

Green

k on RS, p on WS

TULIPS

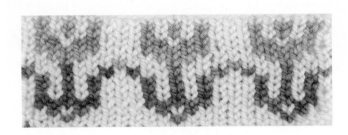

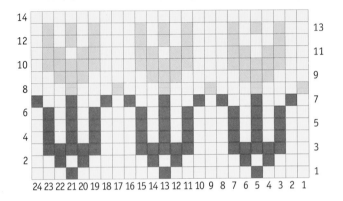

Gold

Pale Yellow

Green

k on RS, p on WS

X AND O

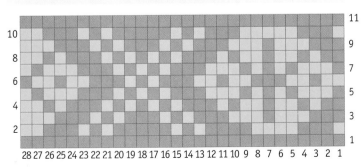

Tan

Gold

k on RS, p on WS

CHAPTER 6

Investigate Intarsia

No color knitting repertoire would be complete without intarsia. The inclusion of areas of contrasting color in knitting creates a look that no other technique can match. In large or small amounts, subtle or stark contrasts, intarsia is what most people think of when they imagine knitting that incorporates pictures. What will you paint?

The intarsia technique enables you to introduce areas of color in any shape, size, and number to the background. Think of these areas as islands floating on the sea of their background. Intarsia fabric is lightweight and fluid because it is only one strand thick. Intarsia pieces are most easily worked flat in rows and seamed. The motifs in this technique are made by following charts.

HOW IT LOOKS

No other knitting technique looks like intarsia. It's easy to recognize by its trademark islands of color, arranged any way the artist wishes, to create pictures in the fabric.

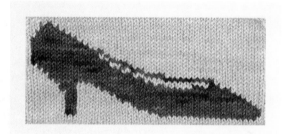

ONE COLOR AT A TIME

Knitted intarsia fabric retains its drape and stretch because the unused colors are not stranded along behind the motifs.

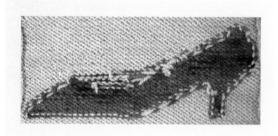

WORK IT FLAT

With rare exceptions, intarsia is worked flat, back and forth in rows. This is due to its special construction. When changing colors, you drop one strand of yarn and leave it hanging for use in the following row (knitting circularly would result in the strand being in the wrong place to continue with on the next row). Don't confuse this with using circular needles; any kind of needle can be used. The important thing is that the work is turned around at the end of each row.

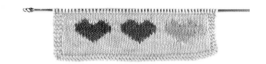

FOLLOW THE CHART

Not unlike a paint-by-numbers canvas, you place the colored stitches in an intarsia design by following a chart row by row. Each row in an intarsia chart follows its own rules, with no restrictions on the number of stitches or colors used.

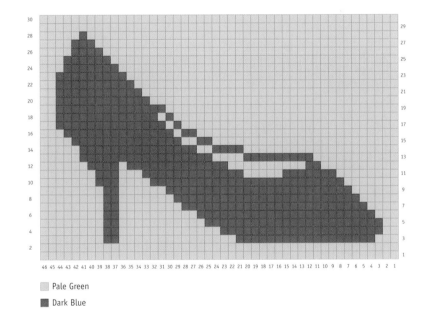

☐ Pale Green
■ Dark Blue

Key Intarsia Points

Creating intarsia calls for you to pay attention to three key points. Once you are comfortable with them, you'll be well on your way to a knitted masterpiece.

COLOR CHANGES

The different areas of color in intarsia are completely separate from each other. The strands not in use are simply abandoned, left hanging until the following row rather than being stranded along behind the work. Every time you change colors, you twist the new strand around the old one, creating interlocks on the wrong side.

YARN SUPPLY

Each color, or area of color, in an intarsia design is worked from its own separate yarn supply. Because there are no rules about how many colors can be in a row of intarsia, there may be many different strands of yarn dangling from your work in any given row. How you handle the various separate yarn sources will depend on your project and your personality.

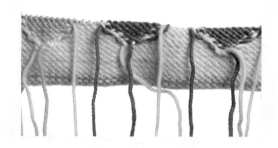

WEAVING IN THE ENDS

Intarsia fabric isn't really finished until its ends are woven in on the wrong side. The many color changes inevitably leave small holes and irregularities in the knitting as you work. Weaving the ends in properly on the back is the secret to perfecting the appearance of the design from the front.

Each time you change colors in an intarsia design, you do it the same way, regardless of whether you are working from the right or wrong side of the piece.

ATTACH A NEW COLOR

Following the chart, work all the stitches you need in the first color. Drop the old strand and forget about it until you need it again in the next row. Tie the new strand around the old one. Work with the new color according to the chart.

CHANGE STRANDS

To change strands, bring the new color up from underneath the old one. This twists the strands together, preventing holes from forming on the front of the work.

TIP

To Knot, or Not

It isn't necessary to knot the strands around one another to keep the knitted fabric secure, because the ends will later be woven in. I advise you to tie knots when adding a new color because it will help you keep an even tension on the new color. Feel free to pick out the knots as you weave in the ends if they bother you. After you have some practice, you may decide you don't need to tie them at all.

Yarn Supply

Each area of color in your design requires its own individual yarn supply, resulting in many strands hanging from your work.

BEFORE OR DURING

Create a new supply of yarn for each area of color as you come to it, or prepare them ahead of time by carefully analyzing your design chart. Either way, the amount of yarn needed for each color island will vary, so just loosely estimate how much length you need.

HOW MUCH YARN

From each main skein of yarn, break off no more than 3 or 4 yards at a time to make a yarn supply. You can add on to a yarn supply if it runs short by splicing (see Chapter 10) or by tying knots.

WRANGLE THE STRANDS

How you control the yarn sources will depend on how many there are, and how long they are. Be careful not to accidentally grab a yarn tail to knit with, rather than the working strand. One way to avoid this is to let all the yarn tails dangle from the front of the work until you are ready to weave them in, and then pull them through to the back side.

Every time you twist the strands around one another at a color change, and again when you turn the work, your yarn source strands will tangle around each other. On the next page are a few ways to manage them. No matter which technique (or combination) you use, your work will look messy while it's in progress.

SEED STITCH PATTERN

Row 1: *K1, p1; rep from * to end of row.

Row 2: Purl the knit sts and knit the purl sts.

Rep Row 2 for patt.

Directions

WORK LOWER FRONT EDGE

With smaller needle and MC, CO 132 (140, 148, 156) sts. Work back and forth in seed st until piece measures 2½" from beg, ending with a WS row.

WORK FRONT BODY

1 With larger needle, work in St st for 4 (8, 12, 16) rows as shown on chart, dec 1 st at end of first row—131 (139, 147, 155) sts.

2 Cont foll chart outline corresponding to your size. Work even, including intarsia motifs as indicated on chart, through Row 134 (136, 138, 140).

SHAPE ARMHOLES

1 BO 7 sts at beg of next 2 rows—117 (125, 133, 141) sts. BO 4 sts at beg of next 2 rows—109 (117, 125, 133) sts. Dec 1 st at each end of next 7 RS rows—95 (103, 111, 119) sts.

2 Work even, foll the chart outline corresponding to your size, to Row 204 (204, 206, 206).

SHAPE NECKLINE AND SHOULDER

1 As indicated on Row 205 (205, 207, 207) of chart, work 35 sts in patt. BO 25 (33, 41, 49) sts, work to end of row—35 sts each side.

2 Cont working on right shoulder only, foll chart. BO 3 sts at beg of next 3 RS rows—26 sts. Dec 1 st at beg of next 5 RS rows—21 sts. Work 2 rows even. BO 7 sts at beg of next 3 WS rows—no sts.

3 Beg with a WS row, reattach working yarn to left shoulder. Cont working in patt according to chart, reversing neckline and shoulder shaping.

WORK LOWER BACK EDGE

With smaller needle and MC, CO 132 (140, 148, 156) sts. Work in seed st until piece measures 2½" from beg, ending with a WS row.

WORK BACK BODY

With larger needle, work back body through Row 134 (136, 138, 140) of chart, dec 1 st at end of first row, foll the chart outline corresponding to your size—131 (139, 147, 155) sts.

SHAPE ARMHOLES

1. Beg with Row 135 (137, 139, 141), BO 7 sts at beg of next 2 rows—117 (125, 133, 141) sts. BO 4 sts at beg of next 2 rows—109 (117, 125, 133) sts. Dec 1 st at each end of next 7 RS rows—95 (103, 111, 119) sts.

2. Work even, following the chart outline corresponding to your size, through row 174. Work intarsia motif as indicated, beg on Row 175.

SHAPE BACK NECKLINE AND SHOULDER

1. As indicated on Row 217 (217, 219, 219) of chart, work 33 sts in patt. BO 29 (37, 45, 53) sts, work to end of row—33 sts each side.

2. Cont working on left shoulder only, foll chart. BO 4 sts at beg of next 3 RS rows—21 sts. BO 7 sts at beg of next 3 WS rows—no sts.

3. Beg with a WS row, reattach working yarn to right shoulder. Cont working according to chart, reversing neckline and shoulder shaping.

MAKE SLEEVE

With larger needle, CO 59 (63, 67, 73) sts. Work in St st for 4 (8, 12, 16) rows, then work intarsia motif as indicated on chart. *At the same time,* inc 1 st at each end of every RS row 7 (8, 10, 11) times—73 (79, 87, 95) sts. Inc 1 st at each end of every other RS row 20 (21, 21, 21) times—113 (121, 129, 137) sts. Work even through Row 112 of chart.

SHAPE SLEEVE CAP

1 Beg with Row 113 of chart, BO 7 sts at beg of next 2 rows—99 (107, 115, 123) sts. BO 4 sts at beg of next 2 rows—91 (99, 107, 115) sts. Dec 1 st at each end of next 20 (19, 18, 18) RS rows—51 (61, 71, 79) sts. BO 2 sts at beg of next 6 (8, 10, 10) rows—39 (45, 51, 59) sts. BO 3 sts at beg of next 2 (0, 2, 2) rows—33 (45, 45, 53) sts. BO 4 sts at beg of next 2 (4, 2, 2) rows. BO rem 25 (29, 37, 45) sts.

2 Make a second sleeve to match, changing color of intarsia motif if desired.

FINISHING

1 Work duplicate st on all pieces as indicated on chart.

2 Weave in ends and block pieces.

3 Sew shoulder seams. Sew body side seams, leaving seed st band at bottom open at sides to form slits.

4 Sew underarm seams on sleeves.

5 With DPN and MC, pick up and knit 58 (62, 66, 72) sts along lower edge of cuff, beg and ending at center of intarsia motif. Working back and forth in rows (to form a slit), work in seed st until cuff measures 2½" from pickup row. BO in patt. Rep for 2nd cuff.

6 With smaller circular needle, pick up and knit 146 (162, 178, 194) sts along neck edge, beg and ending at left shoulder. PM and join for working in rnds. Work in seed st for 6 rnds (about ⅝"). BO in patt.

7 Sew sleeves into armholes.

8 Weave in ends and steam edgings lightly to block.

3

5

Girl's Best Friend Tunic Charts

FRONT CHART

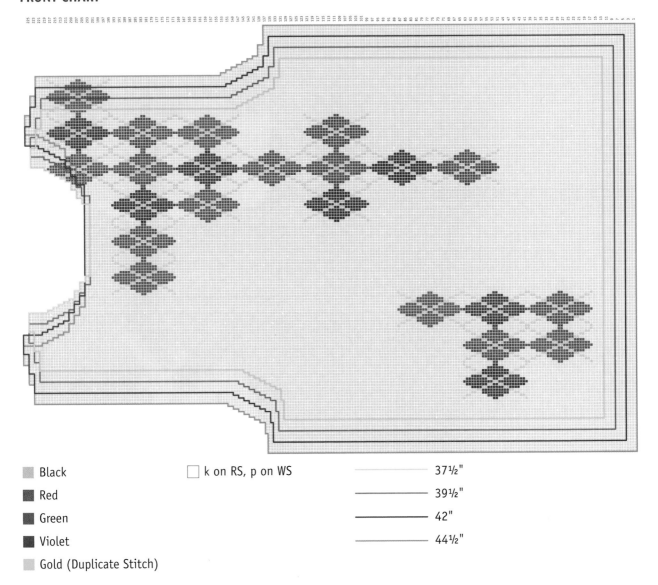

■ Black

■ Red

■ Green

■ Violet

■ Gold (Duplicate Stitch)

□ k on RS, p on WS

37½"

39½"

42"

44½"

BACK CHART

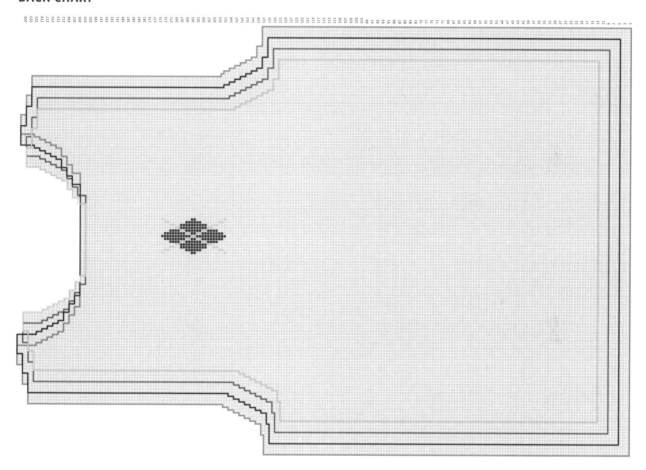

SLEEVE CHART

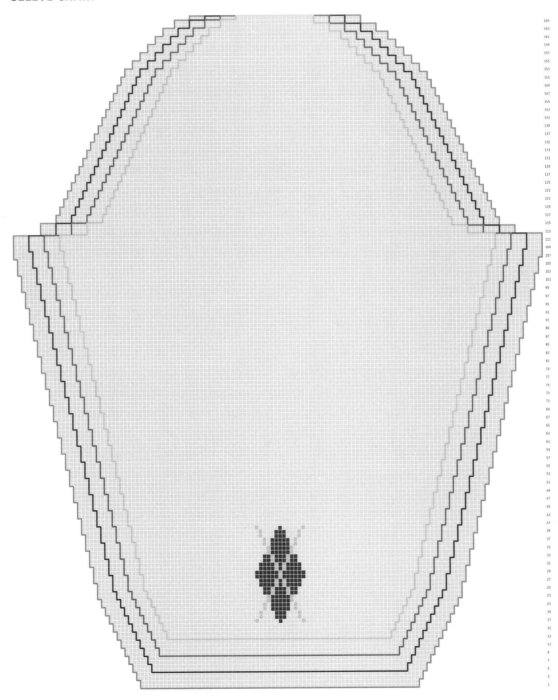

165
163
161
159
157
155
153
151
149
147
145
143
141
139
137
135
133
131
129
127
125
123
121
119
117
115
113
111
109
107
105
103
101
99
97
95
93
91
89
87
85
83
81
79
77
75
73
71
69
67
65
63
61
59
57
55
53
51
49
47
45
43
41
39
37
35
33
31
29
27
25
23
21
19
17
15
13
11
9
7
5
3
1

Girl's Best Friend Tunic Schematic

BODY

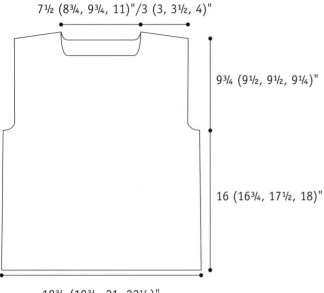

7½ (8¾, 9¾, 11)"/3 (3, 3½, 4)"

9¾ (9½, 9½, 9¼)"

16 (16¾, 17½, 18)"

18¾ (19¾, 21, 22¼)"

SLEEVE

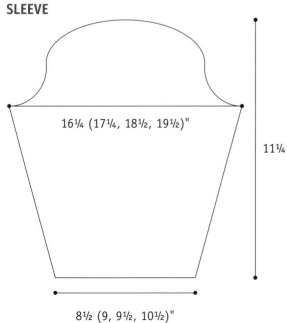

16¼ (17¼, 18½, 19½)"

11¼ (11¾, 12, 12½)"

8½ (9, 9½, 10½)"

Crabby Sweater

Anybody can have One of Those Days, even small people. Here's a sweater that offers fair warning to the world. Cozy and easy to wear, this pullover combines stranded and intarsia techniques with simple stripes and fun rolled edges. A buttoned shoulder opening makes the neckline easy for wee noggins to get through.

Specifications

SIZE
Finished chest measurement: 25½ (27½, 29)", to fit a child

YARN
Sportweight yarn

Shown: Knit Picks *Wool of the Andes Sport,* 100% Peruvian Highland wool, 137 yd./50g

MC: Wonderland Heather, 3 (4, 5) skeins

CC1: Claret Heather, 1 skein

CC2: Avocado, 1 skein

CC3: Marina, 1 skein

CC4: Saffron, 1 skein

CC5: Coal, 1 yd.

GAUGE
26 sts and 36 rows = 4" in St st on larger needle

NEEDLES
Size 3 (3.25mm) 24" circular and DPNs, or size needed to achieve gauge

Size 4 (3.5mm) 24" circular and DPNs, or size needed to achieve gauge

NOTIONS
Stitch marker

Stitch holders

Tapestry needle

Hand sewing needle and thread

Three 1" buttons

CHARTS
For full-size versions of the charts for this pattern, go to www.wiley.com/go/tyvcolorknitting.

Directions

WORK LOWER FRONT EDGE

Foll outline on chart corresponding to your size, with larger needle and CC1, CO 83 (89, 95) sts. Work back and forth in St st for 6 rows. With smaller needle, work 3 rows in k1, p1 rib.

WORK FRONT BODY

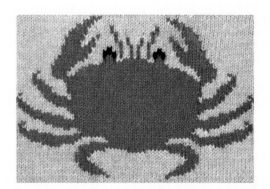

1 Change to larger needle and CC2 and work in St st for 3 rows, as shown on chart. Work waves, as shown on rows 13–24, stranding unused color loosely on WS. Refer to Chapter 5 for tips on stranded colorwork.

2 Cont foll the chart outline corresponding to your size. Work even in MC for 23 (33, 41) rows.

3 Beg with Row 48 of chart, work intarsia motif as shown.

4 Weave in yarn tails around intarsia motif. Work duplicate st eyes in black, as indicated on chart.

SHAPE NECKLINE AND SHOULDERS

1 As indicated on Row 105 (109, 113) of chart, work 30 (28, 26) sts. Work next 23 (33, 43) sts and place them on a holder, work to end of row—30 (28, 26) sts each side.

2 Cont working on right shoulder only. Work dec as foll on the next 3 RS rows: K3, ssk, knit to end of row— 27 (25, 23) sts. Work even for 3 more rows. Place live shoulder sts on holder.

3 Beg with a WS row, reattach working yarn to left shoulder. Cont working according to chart, reversing neckline shaping.

4 Work even for 3 more rows. Next row (RS): Purl. Work 4 rows in St st. BO loosely. Weave in ends and block.

WORK LOWER BACK EDGE

Foll outline on chart corresponding to your size, with larger needle and CC1, CO 83 (89, 95) sts. Work back and forth in St st for 6 rows. With smaller needle, work 3 rows in k1, p1 rib.

WORK BACK BODY

1. With larger needle, change to CC2 and work in St st for 3 rows, as shown on chart. Work waves, as shown on Rows 13–24, stranding unused color loosely on WS. Refer to Chapter 5 for tips on stranded colorwork.

2. Cont foll the chart outline corresponding to your size. Work even to Row 114 (118, 122) of chart.

3. On Row 115 (119, 123), work first 27 (25, 23) sts and place these sts on a holder for right shoulder. Work next 29 (39, 49) sts and place them on a holder for back neck. Work back and forth in k1, p1 rib for 8 rows on rem 27 (25, 23) sts to form under-placket. BO loosely in patt.

4. Weave in ends and block.

MAKE SLEEVE

1. Foll outline on chart corresponding to your size, with larger DPNs, CO 54 (60, 66) sts. PM and join for working in rnds. Work 6 rnds in St st. With smaller DPNs, work 3 rnds in k1, p1 rib.

2. Change to larger DPNs and cont working in patt as indicated on rows 10–24 of chart.

3. Beg with row 25 of chart, inc 1 st at each end of every 5th rnd 11 times as shown on chart—76 (82, 88) sts. Work even for 3 (12, 21) rnds after last inc. BO loosely.

4. Make a second sleeve to match.

5. Weave in ends and block.

FINISHING

❶ With RS tog, join right shoulder using 3-needle BO.

❷ Fold left front placket hem to WS and stitch in place invisibly by hand.

❸ Beg at left placket edge, with smaller needle and CC2, pick up and knit 10 sts along left neck edge, work 23 (33, 43) center front sts from holder, pick up and knit 10 sts along right neck edge, work 29 (39, 49) back neck sts from holder, pick up and knit 10 sts along back left-shoulder under-placket. Work 2 rows in CC2 in St st. Change to CC1 and purl 1 WS row. Work 3 rows in k1, p1 rib. Change to larger needle and work 6 rows in St st. BO loosely.

❹ Make button loops along edge of hemmed placket. Sew buttons to ribbed under-placket, under loops.

❺ Sew sleeves in place, beg at shoulder seam on right and center of placket on left.

❻ Sew side seams. Weave in any rem ends.

Crabby Sweater Charts

FRONT CHART

For Medium and Large sizes, insert 10 (18) more rows MC here

■ Claret

■ Avacado

■ Marina

□ Wonderland Heather

■ Saffron

■ Black (Duplicate Stitch)

□ k on RS, p on WS

─ p on RS, k on WS

———— Small

———— Medium

———— Large

Directions

WORK LOWER FRONT EDGE

Foll chart, with CC1, CO 101 sts using long-tail CO. Work back and forth in garter st for 8 rows.

WORK FRONT BODY

1 Change to MC and work in St st for 2 rows, as shown on chart. Beg with Row 11 of chart, work intarsia patt.

2 When 84 rows of chart are complete, break yarn and place live sts on holder.

3 Weave in ends on WS and steam lightly to block. Sew beads through sequins as shown for eyes.

WORK LOWER BACK EDGE

Foll chart, with CC1, CO 101 sts using long-tail CO. Work back and forth in garter st for 8 rows.

WORK BACK BODY

1 Change to MC and work in St st for 30 rows, as shown on chart. Beg with Row 39 of chart, work intarsia patt.

2 When 84 rows of chart are complete, break yarn and place live sts on holder.

3 Weave in ends on WS and steam lightly to block.

TIP

When working only one or two stitches of a contrasting motif (such as the dragon's claws), it may be easier to strand the yarn across the wrong side of the work than to introduce a different yarn supply.

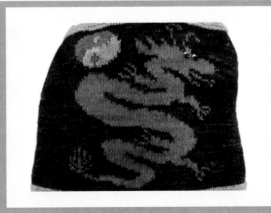

WORK UPPER GARTER BAND

Foll chart and beg with a RS row, change to CC1 and work in garter st across all sts. Without breaking yarn, continue knitting across all sts of front. Join for working in rnds and cont working in garter st for 7 more rnds.

NOTE: To work garter stitch in the round, you must alternate knit and purl rounds.

WORK TOP DECREASES

1. Change to MC and knit 1 rnd, dec 1 st at beg of rnd and another after 100 sts—200 sts.

2. Dec rnd 1: *K18, k2tog, PM; rep from * around—190 sts.

3. Next and every foll alternate rnd: Knit.

4. Dec rnd 2: *Knit to 2 sts before M, k2tog; rep from * around—10 sts dec'd. Rep dec rnd 2 every other rnd 16 more times—20 sts.

5. Next rnd: [K2tog] 10 times—10 sts. Knit 1 rnd. [K2tog] 5 times—5 sts. Break working yarn and thread through tapestry needle. Thread needle through last 5 sts and pull snugly to close. Fasten securely on WS, weaving in end.

MAKE TOP DECORATIONS

1. Ribbon: With CC2, CO 60 sts using long-tail CO. Work back and forth in garter st for 8 rows. BO and weave in ends.

2. Sew coins to ends of ribbon through center holes, as shown, weaving in ends.

3. Top bobble: With MC, CO 6 sts, leaving 18" yarn tail at beg of CO. Work back and forth in St st for 8 rows. Break yarn, leaving 12" tail.

4. Thread tail through tapestry needle. Run needle through live sts, then sew running sts around rem 3 sides of piece. Wind yarn tail from CO into a ball small enough to fit inside piece (wrap around one finger). Place yarn tail ball on WS of piece. Pull working end with tapestry needle to snug bobble around filling. Fasten securely to underside of bobble. Do not break yarn yet.

FINISHING

1 Fold ribbon decoration unevenly. Using tapestry needle still attached to top bobble, stitch bobble to top of tea cozy through folded ribbon. Fasten securely on WS, weaving in ends.

2 Place cozy on teapot to determine optimal placement for side openings.

3 Tack front and back sides of cozy tog with MC under teapot spout and handle, as shown. Weave in yarn tails from tacking sts on WS.

Wulong Tea Cozy Schematic

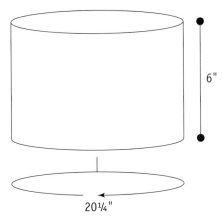

6"

20¼"

Wulong Tea Cozy *(continued)*

FRONT CHART

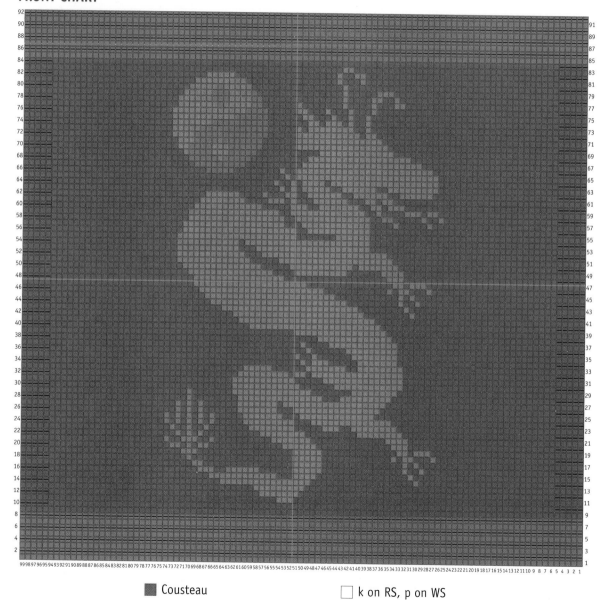

	Cousteau		k on RS, p on WS
	Maple Leaf		p on RS, k on WS
	Tomato		

BACK CHART

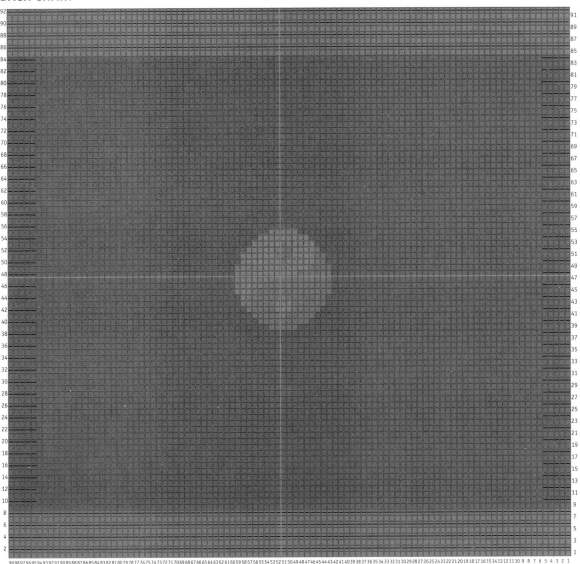

For all motifs in this section, k on RS and p on WS.

AHAAAR-GYLE

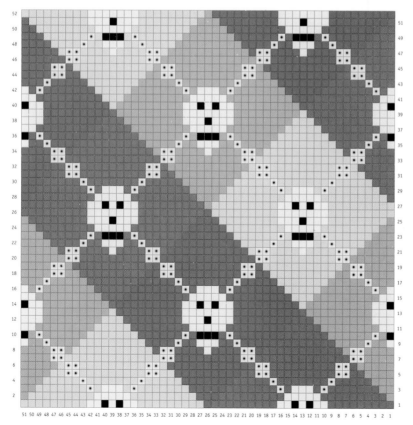

- ■ Gray
- ■ Bright Green
- ■ Dark Green
- ■ Pale Green
- ■ Cream
- ▣ Cream (Duplicate Stitch)
- ■ Black (Duplicate Stitch)

BLUE SUEDE

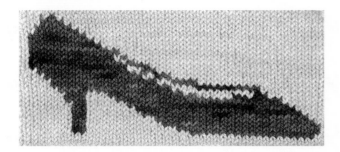

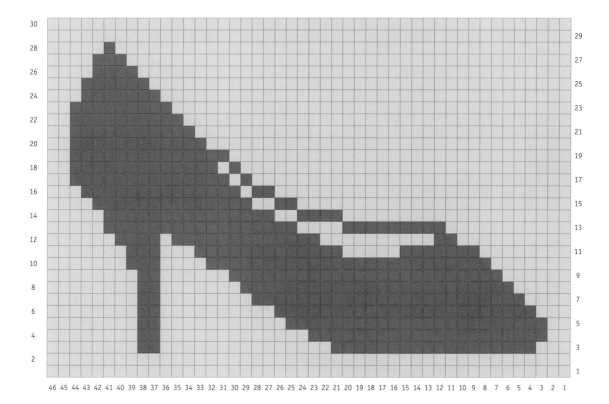

Pale Green

Dark Blue

BUTTERFLY

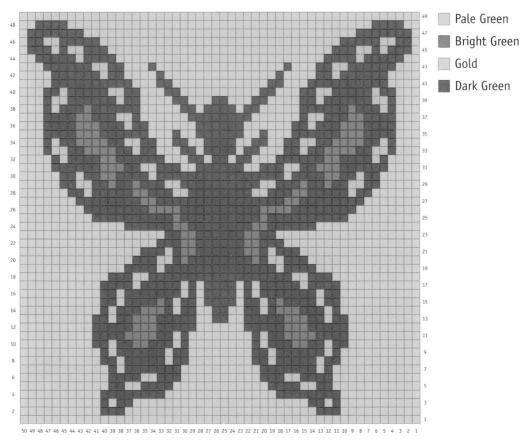

SHEEPISH

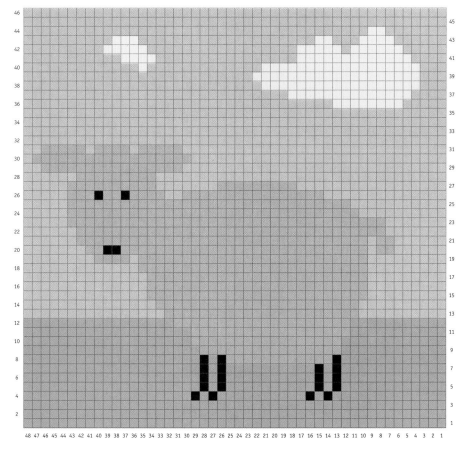

Light Gray

Medium Green

Pale Blue

Cream

Black (Duplicate Stitch)

TEACUP

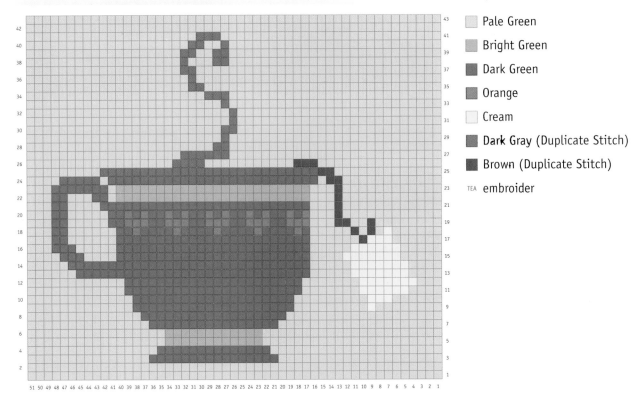

Pale Green

Bright Green

Dark Green

Orange

Cream

Dark Gray (Duplicate Stitch)

Brown (Duplicate Stitch)

TEA embroider

TINY TOWN

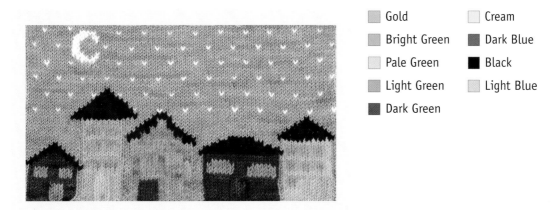

- Gold
- Bright Green
- Pale Green
- Light Green
- Dark Green
- Cream
- Dark Blue
- Black
- Light Blue

CHAPTER 7

Explore Entrelac

For highlighting the best of both color and texture, it's hard to beat entrelac. In addition to the beauty of the finished product, entrelac offers plenty of fun in the execution. Making entrelac is different from any other knitting technique, and many knitters have observed that once you start, it's hard to stop before making "just one more block!"

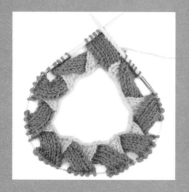  

Think Inside the Blocks

The architecture of entrelac is special, and different from that of other types of knitting. Entrelac fabric is composed of tiers of blocks that are set on their points, forming diamond shapes. Each block is worked individually and joined to its neighbor as it is being knit.

Flat or Circular

Entrelac fabric can be created by knitting either flat or tubular shapes. In either method, you make the individual blocks one at a time by turning the work for each row of stitches.

FLAT ENTRELAC

The vertical edges of flat entrelac knitting require you to insert triangles into its outer edges to create a straight edge.

CIRCULAR ENTRELAC

Because there are no vertical edges in a tube of knitting, side triangles are not needed. You simply join the block at the end of the round to the edge of its neighbor at the beginning.

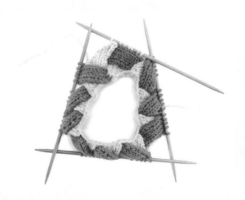

Evenly Knit or Decreased Blocks

There are two types of entrelac blocks: evenly knit and decreased. Evenly knit blocks are for areas of the work where no shaping is needed, while decreased blocks shape the knitting by creating gradually smaller tiers.

EVENLY KNIT

An evenly knit block of entrelac has the same number of stitches at the pick-up (beginning) row as the end. The number of rows in each block depends on the number of stitches in the previous tier's block. Each pair of rows in the current tier joins to a stitch in the previous tier, so there will always be twice as many rows in the current tier of blocks as there are stitches in the previous tier's blocks.

DECREASED

To add shaping to entrelac knitting, the blocks in each tier are knit with either more or fewer stitches than those in the previous one. Most entrelac knitting is worked from bottom to top, probably because decreases usually look neater than increases in the finished fabric.

TIP

Though it's most often shown in stockinette, entrelac blocks can be made in garter stitch as well. Because the shape of garter stitch is more square than rectangular (as in stockinette), garter stitch blocks are more square than stockinette ones—something to consider in your overall design plans.

Knit Circular Entrelac

All of the projects in this chapter are knit in the round, without side triangles. Follow these steps to get started.

Knit a Foundation Tier of Triangles

Entrelac knitting begins with a foundation tier of triangles, from which subsequent tiers of blocks are knit. You cast on the number of stitches needed for the number of blocks required. In this example, each block contains 5 stitches, and each tier contains 10 blocks, so you cast on 50 stitches.

1 Row 1 (WS): P2, turn.

2 Row 2: K2, turn.

3 Row 3: P3, turn.

4 Row 4: K3, turn.

5 Row 5: P4, turn.

6 Cont this patt, adding 1 st on every WS row, until you have 5 total purled sts. Do not turn, but start Row 1 again, purling 2 more sts. Cont across the CO row until all 10 triangles have been formed.

NOTE: Entrelac is different from other knitting in that even when worked circularly, each individual block is still composed of rows, where the work is turned between each one. Therefore it is necessary to differentiate between "Courses" (or "Tiers") which are joined in a circular tube, and "Rows", which are worked back and forth.

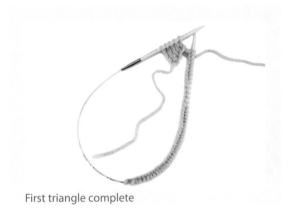

First triangle complete

Ten triangles complete

TIP

Keep your cast-on row of stitches looser than you normally would to preserve the elasticity of the lower edge. Knitted or long-tail cast-ons are good options.

Knit the Second Tier

Each tier of entrelac begins with the opposite side of the work facing you from the last. The first tier of triangles started from the WS, so the next tier of blocks begins on the RS. Break the first color of yarn and join a new one. Join the round of knitting by working your next block along the edge of the first triangle.

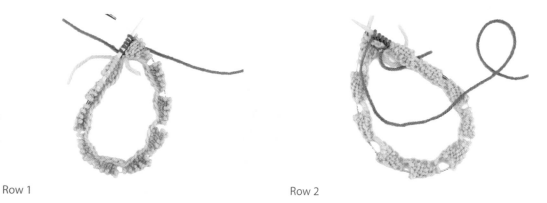

Row 1   Row 2

1 Row 1: At the edge of the first triangle immediately to the right of the beg of the rnd (the first triangle that was created), pick up and knit 5 sts through the triangle's selvedge edge, turn.

2 Row 2: P5, turn.

Row 3   Second tier complete

3 Row 3: K4, ssk (last st with next st of prior color, joining to the triangle), turn. Rep rows 2–3 until all of the triangle sts have been worked into the new rectangle. Work next new block from edge of next triangle to the left.

4 Rep until all the triangles have been worked. The 2nd tier (first tier of blocks) is now complete.

Knit Flat Entrelac

Knitting entrelac flat is the same as knitting it in the round, with one notable difference: The flat piece requires that triangles be inserted along the vertical edges to produce a straight edge.

Work a Right-side Triangle

After completing the foundation tier of triangles as shown at right, break the old yarn and tie in the next color. The first side triangle will be on the right edge of the piece and will begin with the RS facing:

1 Row 1 (RS): K2, turn.

2 Row 2: P2, turn.

3 Row 3: Knit into front and back of st, ssk (1 st from new triangle and 1 from prev tier triangle), turn.

4 Row 4: Purl across triangle, turn.

5 Row 5: Knit into front and back of st, knit to last st of current triangle, ssk, turn.

6 Rep rows 4–5 until all sts of triangle in prev tier have been used. Do not turn after final Row 5. Pick up sts from next adjacent triangle and cont making blocks as for circular entrelac.

Work a Left-side Triangle

When you have filled in the spaces between triangles with a new tier of blocks, you'll need a triangle on the left side to make a straight edge there.

1 Row 1 (RS): Pick up and knit 5 sts along rem edge of last triangle.

2 Row 2: P2tog, purl to end of sts you just picked up, turn.

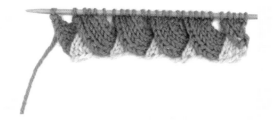

3 Row 3: Knit across, turn.

4 Rep rows 2–3 until 2 sts rem. P2tog, but do not turn. Break yarn, fasten off last st, and tie in a new color. Beg next tier of blocks by picking up 5 sts from selvedge edge of left-side triangle.

TIP

Although the examples here use 5 stitches in each block, you can make your blocks any size you like, depending on the piece you are making and the gauge of your yarn and needles. It's easy to experiment by making swatches with different-sized blocks.

Stained-Glass Stockings

The tops of these Stained-Glass Stockings are a perfect place to try out entrelac. Worked in five tiers of multicolored hand-painted yarn, the woven look of the entrelac blocks highlights the differences between colorways. Rather than incorporating a row of top-row triangles, the stocking tops are bound off to leave the block points intact, creating a sawtooth edge treatment.

Specifications

SIZE

Finished measurements: 16" tall, foot circumference 7½", calf circumference 10½"; sized to fit an adult woman

YARN

Fingering-weight yarn

Shown: Abstract Fiber *Super Sock,* 100% superwash merino, 382 yd.

MC: Cosmopolitan (red), 2 skeins

CC1: Iris (purple/blue/red variegated), 1 skein

CC2: Pinot Noir (wine/green variegated), 1 skein

CC3: Hawthorne Bridge (blue/rust variegated), 1 skein

GAUGE

32 sts and 46 rnds = 4" in St st on smaller needles

NEEDLES

Size 2 (2.75mm) DPNs, or size needed to achieve gauge

Size 3 (3.25mm) 16" circular, or size needed to achieve gauge

NOTIONS

Stitch marker

Tapestry needle

Directions (Make Two)

WORK UPPER EDGE

1 With smaller needles and CC1, CO 72 sts. PM and join for working in rnds.

2 Work in k1, p1 rib until piece measures 1". Knit 1 rnd.

CREATE 6-STITCH FOUNDATION TRIANGLES

1 Row 1 (WS): P2, turn.

2 Row 2: K2, turn.

3 Row 3: P3, turn.

4 Row 4: K3, turn.

5 Row 5: P4, turn.

6 Row 6: K4, turn.

7 Row 7: P5, turn.

8 Row 8: K5, turn.

9 Row 9: P6, do not turn. Beg next triangle, starting again at Row 1. Cont working all the way around until 12 triangles are complete. Break yarn and tie in CC2.

WORK 4 TIERS OF 6-STITCH ENTRELAC BLOCKS

1 Row 1 (RS): Pick up and knit 6 sts through edge of first triangle immediately to right of beg of rnd, turn.

Row 2: P6, turn.

Row 3: K5, ssk (last st of new block plus first st of adjacent triangle), turn.

2 Rep rows 2–3 until all triangle sts have been used, do not turn at end of last row; pick up and knit 6 new sts through next triangle edge.

3 When all 12 CC2 blocks are complete, break yarn and tie ends tog. Join CC3 and work 3rd tier of blocks.

4 When all 12 CC3 blocks are complete, break yarn and tie ends tog. Join CC2 and work 4th tier of blocks.

5 When all 12 CC2 blocks are complete, break yarn and tie ends tog. Join CC1 and work 5th tier of blocks.

BIND OFF SAWTOOTH EDGE

With larger circular needle and RS facing, *k5, knit into f, b, f, and b of next st (make 4 sts from 1), pick up and knit 6 sts. Rep from * 11 more times. BO.

KNIT STOCKING

1 With smaller DPNs and MC, working from WS of stocking top, pick up and knit 72 sts through plain knitted rnd between ribbing and entrelac. PM and join for working in rnds.

NOTE: WS of entrelac cuff must face RS of stocking.

2 Work 3 rnds even.

WORK CALF INCREASES

1 Inc rnd: *K2, M1L, work to last 2 sts, M1R, k2. Rep inc rnd every 4th rnd 5 more times—84 sts.

2 Work even for 1½".

WORK LEG DECREASES

Dec rnd: *K1, ssk, work to last 3 sts, k2tog, k1. Rep dec rnd every 4th rnd 11 more times—60 sts. Work even until stocking measures 12¼" from top of rib, ending last rnd 15 sts before end of rnd.

WORK FIRST TIER OF 12-STITCH BLOCKS

1 Next row (RS): Pick up and knit 12 sts through selvedge edge of first triangle on right needle.

2 Row 1: P12, turn.

3 Row 2: K11, ssk (last st of block with next st of triangle), turn.

4 Rep rows 1 and 2 until all triangle sts have been used and 24 rows have been worked. Rep until 10 blocks have been worked. Break yarn and tie ends tog. Join CC3.

WORK NEXT TIER OF 11-STITCH BLOCKS

1 Next row (WS): Pick up and purl 12 sts from edge of adjoining block.

2 Row 1: K2tog, k10, turn—11 sts.

3 Row 2: P10, p2tog (last st of block with next st of adjoining block from prev tier), turn.

4 Row 3: K11, turn.

5 Rep rows 2 and 3 until all sts of adjoining block from prev tier have been used and 24 rows have been worked, ending with Row 2. Rep until 10 blocks have been worked. Break yarn and tie ends tog. Join MC.

CONTINUE WORKING NEW TIERS, DECREASING BY 1 STITCH WITH EACH

1. Work next tier with MC, from RS, and with blocks of 10 sts and 22 rows each. Break yarn, tie ends tog, and join CC1.

2. Work next tier with CC1, from WS, and with blocks of 9 sts and 20 rows each. Break yarn, tie ends tog, and join CC2.

3. Work next tier with CC2, from RS, and with blocks of 8 sts and 18 rows each. Break yarn, tie ends tog, and join CC3.

4. Work next tier with CC3, from WS, and with blocks of 7 sts and 16 rows each. Break yarn, tie ends tog, and join MC.

5. Work next tier with MC, from RS, and with blocks of 6 sts and 14 rows each. Break yarn, tie ends tog, and join CC1.

Dahlia Tote from WS

6. Work next tier with CC1, from WS, and with blocks of 5 sts and 12 rows each. Break yarn, tie ends tog, and join CC2.

7. Work next tier with CC2, from RS, and with blocks of 4 sts and 10 rows each. Break yarn, tie ends tog, and join CC3.

8. Work next tier with CC3, from WS, and with blocks of 3 sts and 8 rows each. Break yarn, tie ends tog, and join MC.

9. Work next tier with MC, from RS, and with blocks of 2 sts and 6 rows each. Break yarn, tie ends tog, and join CC1.

10. Work last tier with CC1, from WS, and with blocks of 1 st and 4 rows each.

CLOSE BAG BOTTOM

1 Next rnd (RS): [K2tog] 5 times—5 sts.

2 Break yarn and thread end through tapestry needle. Run through last 5 sts and pull gently to gather. Fasten securely on WS.

FINISHING

1 Pick out CO sts from cord end and remove waste yarn from opposite end. Graft ends of cord tog.

2 Wash tote in washing machine, using hottest water available, as many times as needed to felt fully. Dry in clothes dryer.

3 Sew straps to bag, foll manufacturer's instructions.

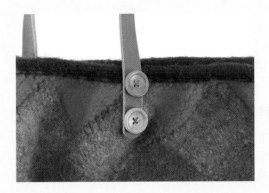

TIP

For better felting, place the tote inside a mesh laundry bag and add a pair of jeans and either a pair of sneakers or a few tennis balls to the machine. Put the jeans and sneakers or tennis balls in the dryer with the tote as well.

Kaleidoscope Tam

The art of entrelac knitting has experienced a revival in popularity with the advent of long-repeat self-striping yarns. The Kaleidoscope Tam shows why: As the colors change along the length of each strand of yarn, every block of knitting takes on its own personality. The corrugated rib band provides a jaunty base for the woven diamonds, and a whimsical stem on top finishes the look.

Specifications

SIZE
Band circumference: 20 (21¼)"

YARN
Worsted-weight yarn

Shown: Knit One Crochet Too *Paint Box,* 100% wool, 100 yd.

MC: #1 Thistle (lavender/green variegated), 2 skeins

CC: #12 Tandoor (rust variegated), 2 skeins

GAUGE
22 sts and 32 rows = 4" in St st on larger needle

NEEDLES
Size 5 (3.75mm) 16" circular, or size needed to achieve gauge

Size 6 (4mm) 16" circular and DPNs, or size needed to achieve gauge

NOTIONS
Stitch marker

Tapestry needle

Directions

WORK BAND

1. With smaller needle and MC, CO 120 (128) sts. PM and join for working in rnds.

2. Tie in CC and work in corrugated rib (k2 with MC, p2 with CC) until piece measures 1½". Break off CC.

WORK FOUNDATION TIER OF 8-STITCH TRIANGLES

Change to larger needle and cont with MC.

1. Row 1 (WS): P2, turn.

2. Row 2: K2, turn.

3. Row 3: P3, turn.

4. Row 4: K3, turn.

5. Cont adding sts in this way until triangle reaches 8 sts on WS (13 rows total); do not turn at end of last row. Begin again with Row 1.

6. Cont until 15 (16) triangles have been made. Break yarn and knot ends tog. Join CC.

WORK FIRST TIER OF 8-STITCH BLOCKS

1. Next row (RS): Pick up and knit 8 sts through selvedge edge of first triangle on right needle.

2. Row 1: P8, turn.

3. Row 2: K7, ssk (last st of block with next st of triangle), turn.

4. Rep rows 1 and 2 until all triangle sts have been used and 16 rows have been worked.

5. Rep until 15 (16) blocks have been worked. Break yarn and tie ends tog. Join MC.

WORK SECOND TIER OF 8-STITCH BLOCKS

1. Next row (WS): Pick up and purl 8 sts through selvedge edge of next adjoining block from prev tier.

2. Row 1: K8, turn.

3. Row 2: P7, p2tog (last st of current block with next st of block from prev tier), turn.

4. Rep rows 1 and 2 until all sts of block from prev tier have been used, and 16 rows have been worked.

5. Rep until 15 (16) blocks have been worked. Break yarn and tie ends tog. Join CC.

WS

WORK NEXT TIER WITH 7-STITCH BLOCKS

1. Next row (RS): Pick up and knit 8 sts from edge of adjoining block.

2. Row 1: P2tog, p6, turn—7 sts.

3. Row 2: K6, ssk (last st of block with next st of adjoining block from prev tier), turn.

4. Row 3: P7, turn.

5. Rep rows 2 and 3 until all sts of adjoining block from prev tier have been used, and 16 rows have been worked, ending with Row 2.

6. Rep until 15 (16) blocks have been worked. Break yarn and tie ends tog. Join MC.

RS

CONTINUE WORKING NEW TIERS, DECREASING BY 1 STITCH WITH EACH

1. Work next tier with MC, from WS, and with blocks of 6 sts and 14 rows each. Break yarn, tie ends tog, and join CC.

2. Work next tier with CC, from RS, and with blocks of 5 sts and 12 rows each. Break yarn, tie ends tog, and join MC.

3. Work next tier with MC, from WS, and with blocks of 4 sts and 10 rows each. Break yarn, tie ends tog, and join CC.

4. Work next tier with CC, from RS, and with blocks of 3 sts and 8 rows each. Break yarn, tie ends tog, and join MC.

5. Work next tier with MC, from WS, and with blocks of 2 sts and 6 rows each. Break yarn, tie ends tog, and join CC.

WORK FINAL TIER

1 With CC, working from RS, [k1, pick up and knit 1 st from side of block in prev tier] 15 (16) times—30 (32) sts.

2 Next rnd: Knit.

3 Next rnd: [K2tog] 15 (16) times—15 (16) sts.

4 Next rnd: Knit.

5 Next rnd: [K2tog] 7 (8) times, k1 (0)—8 sts.

WORK TOP STEM

1 Break yarn and tie in MC. Knit 1 rnd.

2 Next rnd: [K2tog] 4 times—4 sts.

3 Work 4-st knitted cord for 1". Break yarn and thread through tapestry needle. Run yarn tail through last 4 sts and fasten. Draw yarn tail into stem and trim from WS.

FINISHING

Weave in yarn tails and block.

Kaleidoscope Tam Schematic

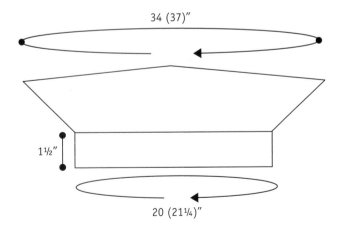

34 (37)"

1½"

20 (21¼)"

CHAPTER 8

Make Modules

Rediscover the joy of playing with blocks. Modular knitting is geometric in the purest sense. It's based on simple shapes that are joined together into units, then finished pieces. The shapes you choose, the methods you use to join them, and the yarn you select all combine to create the design. Like puzzles with many pieces, modular designs are greater than the sums of their parts.

Modular Construction

M odular designs rely on the smaller pieces from which they are constructed for their shaping, and their overall silhouettes. The simplicity of this construction enables knitters to create unique designs without following a pattern. Instead, you simply choose the shape(s) on which your project will be based and plan its construction from there.

CHOOSE A SHAPE

What shapes inspire you? The tidy angles of squares? The dynamic intersections of triangles? The fluid curves of circles? Pick the shapes that speak to you.

JOIN SHAPES INTO UNITS

Repeat the shapes you've chosen in different colors, arrange them in different directions, or simply create a profusion of them. Then connect them into groups, or *modules,* for placement within the design.

JOIN UNITS INTO GARMENTS

Connect the modules into a completed project by joining them with seams or by picking up and knitting into them.

Shapes connected in modules

The shapes you select determine the direction of your design. Base your selection on the yarn you're using, the stitch you want to knit, or the shape you most enjoy knitting (you'll need many of them, so select geometrics you like making). Any shape or combination of shapes is fair game in modular knitting. Here are a few examples.

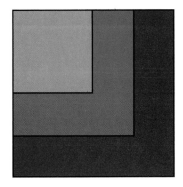

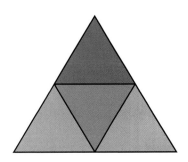

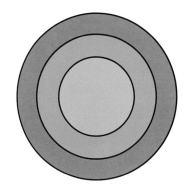

SQUARES AND RECTANGLES

Right angles are incredibly versatile. Squares, diamonds, and rectangles of any size or combination work well together and are simple to join.

TRIANGLES

Both right and equilateral triangles are great candidates for modular knitting. Turn them in any direction to make interesting combinations. The points of triangles naturally enable you to direct attention to key areas within your design.

CURVES

Circles, fans, and spirals make fascinating modular knitting. Their rounded edges echo the curves of human bodies, making them natural choices for feminine looks. The fullness at the edge of a circle or curve is easy to use as a ruffle or flounce.

TIP

The placement and orientation of modules can be used to play up or down any features you want, so use them to best advantage. But be careful; you may want to evaluate where those triangles are pointing!

A fter you've knit your shapes, you join them into units, creating modules.

COLOR CHANGES

In addition to the geometry of your modules, their colors have great impact on the finished look of the piece. Plan your units to repeat the same progression of colors, or toss them randomly into place. Just as when you look through a kaleidoscope, the repetition and placement of color changes the look of the shapes you have chosen.

MODULE SIZE

The size of each module, after its separate parts are joined, impacts your overall design. Does your piece look better with a few large areas of color or with many smaller parts?

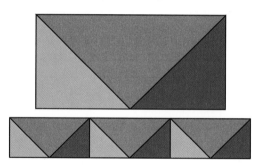

DIRECTION

One interesting aspect of modular knitting is that you can change the direction, or *grain,* of different shapes within each module. Try running your knitting crosswise or on the diagonal to play up the characteristics of the yarn you are working with.

WORK TOP-EDGE TRIANGLES

Top-edge triangles are worked in one color.

TRIANGLE 42

1. With new color, knit live st from Block 41, pick up and knit 14 sts along top-left edge of Block 41, 1 st from center of Block 35, 1 st from upper-right edge of Triangle 36. Turn work.

2. Row B (WS): P2tog, p to end of row.

3. Row A (RS): Sl1 kwise, ssk, work to end of row, pick up and knit 1 st from upper-right edge of Triangle 36.

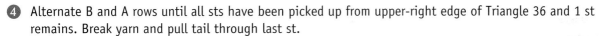

4. Alternate B and A rows until all sts have been picked up from upper-right edge of Triangle 36 and 1 st remains. Break yarn and pull tail through last st.

5. Rep for Blocks 46 and 48.

FINISHING

1. Weave in ends. Felt piece in washing machine and dryer.

2. Fold bag with RS tog and sew side seams with hand sewing needle and thread.

3. Turn bag RS out. Beg at top edge under flap, sew trim along top edge and around flap edge, forming loop to fit button at point of flap.

4. Sew button under loop.

5. Sew shoulder strap in place.

NOTE: See Chapter 10 for instructions on how to make Dorset buttons.

Chevrons Shoulder Bag Schematic

12"

MC Purple

CC1 Blue

CC2 Black

CC3 Red

CC4 Pink

CC5 Green

30"

42 CC4	46 CC5	48 MC
36 CC3 & CC1	41 CC1 & MC	45 CC4 & CC3	47 CC1 & CC2
35 CC5 & CC2	40 CC2 & CC3	444 CC4 & CC5
29 MC & CC4	34 CC4 & CC1	39 CC1 & MC	43 CC2 & CC5
28 CC2 & CC3	33 CC5 & CC1	38 CC3 & CC4
22 CC5 & CC1	27 CC3 & MC	32 CC2 & CC4	37 CC1 & MC
21 CC4 & CC5	26 MC & CC1	31 CC3 & CC5
15 CC1 & MC	20 CC2 & CC5	25 CC4 & CC1	30 CC3 & CC2
14 CC1 & CC4	19 CC3 & MC	24 CC5 & MC
9 CC3 & CC5	13 CC5 & CC1	18 CC1 & CC2	28 CC2 & CC3
8 CC1 & CC2	12 CC4 & CC5	17 MC & CC4
4 CC4 & CC3	7 CC3 & CC1	11 CC2 & CC3	16 CC5 & CC1
3 CC2 & CC5	6 CC5 & MC	10 CC4 & CC3
	2 CC1 & CC4	5 CC1 & CC2
	1 MC & CC3	

Fom a ram's horn to a nautilus shell to the center of a rose, spirals are everywhere in nature. Combining five colorways of hand-painted yarn, this skirt draws on the strengths of the spiral: energy, motion, and decreasing diagonal lines that flatter the figure. The construction is simple and fun. Work the number of modules for your size, and then seam together. Instant spirals!

Specifications

SIZE
Finished hip circumference: 40½ (45, 49½, 54)"

YARN
Shown: Abstract Fiber *Calder,* 100% superwash merino wool, 330 yd., 4 oz

MC: Joseph's Coat, 1 skein

CC1: Smith Rock, 1 skein

CC2: Hopworks, 1 skein

CC3: Marionberry, 1 skein

CC4: Black Opal, 1 skein

GAUGE
26 sts and 34 rows = 4" in St st

NEEDLES
Size 4 (3.5mm) 32" circular, or size needed to achieve gauge

NOTIONS
Stitch marker

Tapestry needle

1"-wide elastic, length of waist measurement plus 1"

Hand-sewing needle and thread

Directions

WORK LOWER EDGE TRIANGLES

1 With MC, CO 21 sts.

2 Row A (WS): Purl 1 row.

3 Row B (RS): K1, ssk, knit to last 3 sts, k2tog, k1.

4 Alternate A and B rows until 5 sts rem. K1, sl1, k2tog, psso, k1—3 sts. Purl 1 row.

5 Next row: Sl1, k2tog, psso. Break yarn, leaving last st live for reuse.

6 With CC1, pick up and knit 20 sts, beg at lower-right edge of Triangle 1, knit last live st from Triangle 1—21 sts.

7 Rep from Step 1 to form Triangle 2.

8 Change to CC2 and rep Step 2, then Step 1, to form Triangle 3.

WORK SPIRAL

1 With CC3, pick up and knit 43 sts along long edge of triangles module. Purl 1 row.

2 Work bias St st rows.

3 Row A (RS): K1, M1R, knit to last 3 sts, k2tog, k1.

4 Row B (WS): Purl.

5 Alternate A and B rows until piece measures 5 (5½, 6, 6½)" from beg, ending with a B row.

6 Next row (RS): Work to center 3 sts, sl1, k2tog, psso, work to end of row. Rep centered double dec every 22nd row, 7 more times—27 sts. Purl 1 row. Place live sts on holder.

TIP

To accurately measure the length of your spiral module, first lay it flat. Then place a ruler with its end at the bottom edge of the center triangle and its edge parallel to one column of stitches.

MAKE ALL THE MODULES FOR YOUR SIZE

1. Using 4 different colors each time, make 8 (9, 10, 11) more modules.

2. Weave in ends and block each module.

SEAM MODULES

1. Arrange all modules into the color progression you like best.

2. Working from bottom to top, seam modules together with tapestry needle and mattress st. Open spaces should form between the triangle modules, as shown.

3. Weave in ends and steam lightly to block seams.

MAKE WAISTBAND

1. Place 243 (270, 297, 324) live sts around top edge on circular needle. With CC4, work in St st for 1¼". Purl 1 row for a turning edge. Work 1¼" in St st. BO.

2. Fold waistband to WS along purl row and pin in place. Sew in place by hand, invisibly from WS, leaving a 1" opening to insert elastic.

3. Draw elastic through waistband using a safety pin. Overlap ends by 1" and sew securely together. Sew opening in waistband closed.

TIP

When seaming the modules together, try using the knitted or crochet joining techniques to add a new color and emphasize the diagonal lines in this garment.

Spiral Skirt Schematic

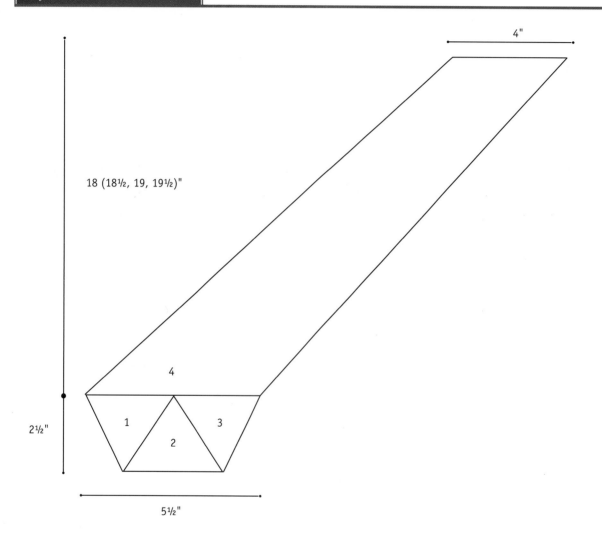

GARTER SQUARE

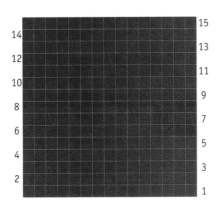

k every st, every row

CORNER-MITERED SQUARE

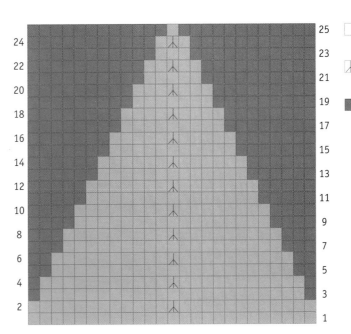

k on WS,
p on WS

sl 2 sts kwise,
k1, p2sso

no stitch

CENTER-MITERED SQUARE

CO 8 sts. Arrange evenly on DPNs and join for working in rnds. PM in 1st, 3rd, 5th, and 7th sts.

Rnd 1: Purl.

Rnd 2: *YO, k1, rep from * to end of rnd—16 sts.

Rnd 3: Purl.

Rnd 4: Knit, making a YO before and after each marked st.

Rep rnds 3 and 4 to desired size. BO. Close gaps by darning in yarn tails.

EQUILATERAL TRIANGLE

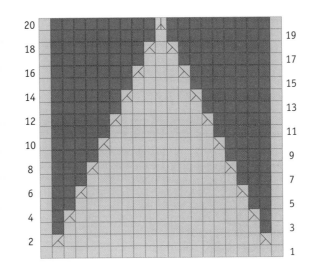

	k on RS, p on WS
⧅	ssk
⧄	k2tog
⬛	no stitch
⋏	sl 2 kwise, k1, p2sso

RIGHT TRIANGLE, RIGHT-LEANING

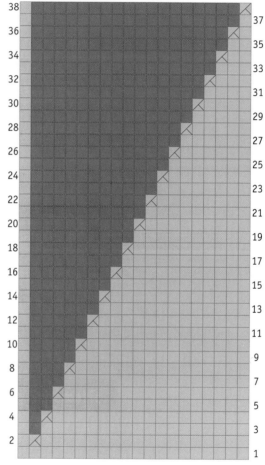

- ☐ k on RS, p on WS
- ☒ k2tog
- ■ no stitch

RIGHT TRIANGLE, LEFT-LEANING

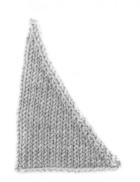

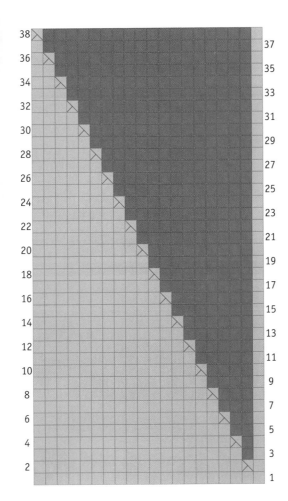

k on RS, p on WS

k2tog

no stitch

GARTER SCALLOP

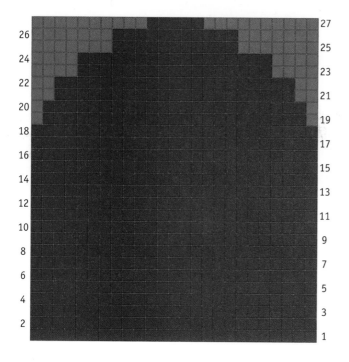

☐ k every st, every row

■ BO at beg of each row as shown

STOCKINETTE CIRCLE

CO 8 sts. Place evenly on DPNs and join for working in rnds.

Rnd 1: Knit.

Rnd 2: *K1, M1L, rep from * to end of rnd—16 sts.

Rnd 3: Knit.

Rnd 4: *K2, M1L, rep from * to end of rnd—24 sts.

Rnd 5: Knit.

Rnd 6: *K3, M1L, rep from * to end of rnd—32 sts.

Rnd 7: Knit.

Rnd 8: *K4, M1L, rep from * to end of rnd—40 sts.

Rnd 9: Knit.

Rnd 10: *K5, M1L, rep from * to end of rnd—48 sts.

Rnds 11–12: Knit.

Continue in this manner, adding 1 additional knit st between increases in each subsequent inc rnd and working 2 knit rnds after every 5 inc rnds, until circle reaches desired size. BO loosely after an inc rnd. Close gaps by darning in yarn tails.

PARALLELOGRAM

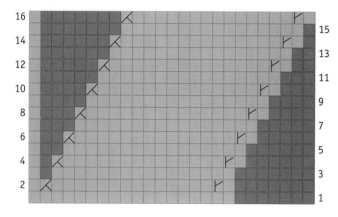

☐	k on RS, p on WS	
╱	k2tog	
⌐	k into f & b	
■	no stitch	

HEXAGON

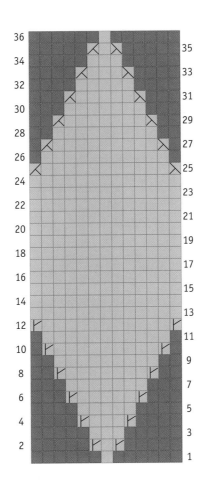

☐	k every st, every row
Ͱ	k into f & b
⧄	k2tog
⧅	sSK
⬛	no stitch

BIAS RECTANGLE

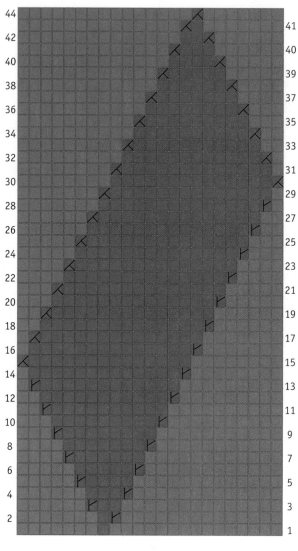

	k every st, every row
	k into f & b
	k2tog
	no stitch

TRAPEZOID

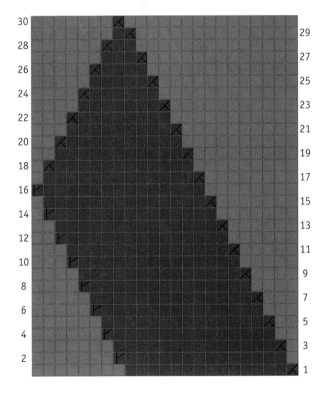

Symbol	Description
☐	k every st, every row
Ⱶ	k into f & b
⧄	k2tog
■	no stitch

CHAPTER 9

Embrace Embellishment

Want to enhance simply-knit pieces with extra color? Add whimsy and flair to traditional garments? Embellishment is the answer. Like punctuation marks, surface accents provide the finishing highlights to your knitting. Embellishment sets the mood, showcases your yarn, and emphasizes your personal style.

Embellishment As the Icing on the Cake

Cake all by itself is great, but the addition of icing takes dessert to a whole new level. In addition to adding flavor, icing changes the entire look and style of the cake. Think of embellishments the same way: you can use them to highlight your knitting's best features, underscore a design theme, or even let them become the main attraction of the piece.

Functional or Decorative?

Embellishments can be as obvious or subtle as you like. Think first about what type of accent your piece calls for.

FUNCTIONAL
Closures, edgings, flaps, and ties are examples of functional elements in knitting. They can also be used as embellishments, pulling double duty by also adding style.

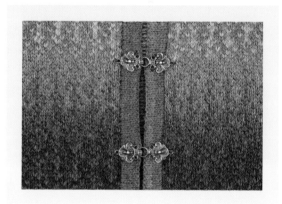

DECORATIVE
Tassels, trims, bobbles, and bows are purely decorative. You can use them to enhance other details or add a whole new element to knitted designs.

Three Embellishment Types

Almost anything can be an embellishment to your knitting. As you compose your knitted piece, consider these varieties of decoration:

STRUCTURAL

Edges (like the knitted cord shown at right), seams, and shaping are parts of even the simplest knitted pieces. Think about making one or more of these areas decorative rather than purely functional.

INTEGRAL

Anything that is knitted into the piece, rather than attached at the end, is an integral embellishment. The overall pattern in your knitted fabric (such as these cables) is one integral embellishment. So are the yarn colors you choose. Flaps, bands, and closures are all opportunities to embellish your work.

APPLIED

Buttons, beads, pompoms, and cords are examples of applied accents. Any piece that is attached after the knitting is complete counts as an applied embellishment.

TIP

Embellishments can be very understated: a slender cord, a perfectly matched button, an invisible hem. All contribute to the overall polish of your design without calling attention to themselves.

The way you incorporate embellishments into your design depends on the intended use of the piece, its method of construction, and how you make the embellishments.

EDGINGS

Often, one of the first decisions you make about your knitting is what sort of edging you'll use. An integral embellishment, the edging you choose can be as simple as a rolled hem or as elaborate as a lace cuff. Take your time considering how different edgings create different moods for your design.

YARN ADORNMENTS

Tassels, cords, flowers, stems, and leaves are all made of yarn—either the same as that used for the main body of your design or something contrasting. Applied yarn decorations have the advantage of looking organic to the rest of the piece, being made from the same substance.

TIP

Don't forget about elasticity when you select decorative treatments. Generally speaking, wrists, ankles, necklines, and waistbands need to retain their stretch. Choose other locations for decorations that could inhibit elasticity.

SEWING

You affix buttons, ribbons, sequins, and beads to knitting with a needle and thread. You almost never attach embellishments to hand-knitted garments with a sewing machine, because the sewing usually needs to be done invisibly. Most embellishment sewing is no more challenging than sewing on a button.

EMBROIDERY

Most embroidery stitches are easy to execute and look much more intricate than they really are. Embroidery has the advantage of scale on its side: you can make your embellishments exactly the proper size for the piece you are working on. Floss, cord, silk ribbon, and, of course, yarn are all beautiful when applied to knitting—if you can fit it through the eye of a needle, you can embroider your knitting with it.

TIP

Need some embroidery practice before you work on your newly finished knitting? Grab some knitted items from garage sales and secondhand stores to experiment on.

Rose Garden Cloche

Long-repeat self-striping yarn can make magic when you use it for applied surface accents. The trick is to knit the hat, breaking off lengths of each color for future use as you come to them. Skeins like this one, which are engineered to begin and end with the same colors each time, make it easy. A lacy edging and openwork spiral decreases further complement this cabbage rose appliqué, with its millinery-style bow detail.

Specifications

SIZE
Finished circumference: 21¾"

YARN
Sportweight yarn

Shown: Freia Fine Handpaint Yarns *Rustic Ombré Sport Wool,* 100% wool, 217 yd.

Melon, 1 ball

GAUGE
28 sts and 42 rnds = 4" in St st

NEEDLES
Size 3 (3.25mm) 16" circular and DPNs, or size needed to achieve gauge

NOTIONS
Stitch markers

Tapestry needle

Sewing needle and thread

Directions

WORK LOWER EDGE

1 CO 304 sts using cable CO. PM and join for working in rnds. Next rnd: *K7, pass 2nd, 3rd, 4th, 5th, 6th, and 7th sts on right needle over first st, yo, k1, yo; rep from * to end of rnd—152 sts. Knit 1 rnd, ending 1 st before end of rnd. PM for new beg of rnd (remove old M when you come to it). Next rnd: *Sl1, k2tog, psso, yo, k1, yo; rep from * to end of rnd. [Knit 1 rnd, purl 1 rnd] 3 times.

WORK MAIN BODY

1 Work even in St st until piece measures 4" from CO, breaking off 4 yd. of yellow and 5 yd. of orange, when possible.

2 As you work, the color of the yarn will slowly change. When the strand is mostly yellow, break off 4 yds for later use. Rejoin the ends and continue.

3 When the strand is mostly orange, break off 5 yds for later use. Rejoin the ends and continue.

WORK SPIRAL DECREASES

1 Work decs every other rnd as foll:

2 Rnd 1: *K15, k2tog, yo, k2tog; rep from * to end of rnd—144 sts.

3 Rnd 3: K13, k2tog, yo, k2tog, *k14, k2tog, yo, k2tog; rep from * to last st, k1—136 sts.

4 Rnd 5: K11, k2tog, yo, k2tog, *k13, k2tog, yo, k2tog; rep from * to last 2 sts, k2—128 sts.

5 Rnd 7: K9, k2tog, yo, k2tog, *k12, k2tog, yo, k2tog; rep from * to last 3 sts, k3—120 sts.

6 Rnd 9: K7, k2tog, yo, k2tog, *k11, k2tog, yo, k2tog; rep from * to last 4 sts, k4—112 sts.

7 Rnd 11: K5, k2tog, yo, k2tog, *k10, k2tog, yo, k2tog; rep from * to last 5 sts, k5—104 sts.

8 Rnd 13: K3, k2tog, yo, k2tog, *k9, k2tog, yo, k2tog; rep from * to last 6 sts, k6—96 sts.

9 Rnd 15: K1, k2tog, yo, k2tog, *k8, k2tog, yo, k2tog; rep from * to last 7 sts, k7—88 sts.

10 Rnd 16: Knit to last st, PM for new beg of rnd (remove old M when you come to it).

11 Rnd 17: K2tog, yo, k2tog, *k7, k2tog, yo, k2tog; rep from * to last 7 sts, k7—80 sts.

12 Rnd 19: K2tog, *k6, k2tog, yo, k2tog; rep from * to last 8 sts, k6, k2tog, yo—72 sts.

⓭ Rnd 21: *K5, k2tog, yo, k2tog; rep from * to end of rnd—64 sts.

⓮ Rnd 23: K3, k2tog, yo, k2tog, *k4, k2tog, yo, k2tog; rep from * to last st, k1—56 sts.

⓯ Rnd 25: K1, k2tog, yo, k2tog, *k3, k2tog, yo, k2tog; rep from * to last 2 sts, k2—48 sts.

⓰ Rnd 26: Knit to last st, PM for new beg of rnd (remove old M when you come to it).

⓱ Rnd 27: K2tog, yo, k2tog, *k2, k2tog, yo, k2tog; rep from * to last 2 sts, k2—40 sts.

⓲ Rnd 29: K2tog, *k1, k2tog, yo, k2tog; rep from * to last 3 sts, k1, k2tog, yo—32 sts.

⓳ Rnd 31: *K2tog, yo; rep from * to end of rnd.

⓴ Rnd 33: *K2tog; rep from * to end of rnd—16 sts.

㉑ Rnd 35: *K2tog; rep from * to end of rnd—8 sts.

㉒ Break yarn and thread through tapestry needle. Run needle through last 8 sts and pull snug. Fasten securely and weave in end on WS.

LARGE LEAF CHART

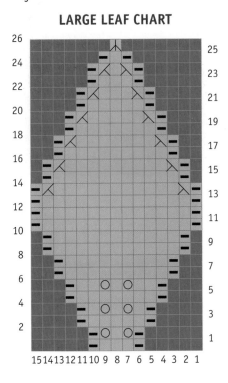

SMALL LEAF CHART

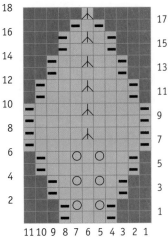

□	k on RS, p on WS
⊟	p on RS, k on WS
○	yo
◹	k2tog
◸	ssk
◭	sl2 knitwise, k1, p2 sso

❶ (When green is the first color on the ball): Make 3 large leaves, foll the Large Leaf Chart.

❷ Make 2 small leaves, foll the Small Leaf Chart.

228

MAKE REMAINING APPLIQUÉS

CENTER CHART

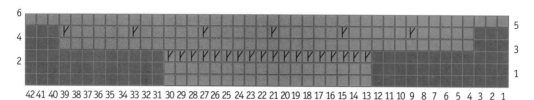

SMALL PETAL CHART

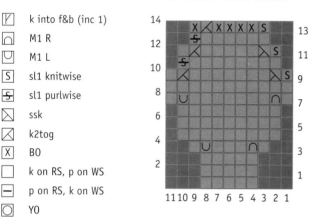

LARGE PETAL CHART

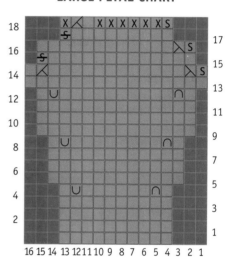

⤶	k into f&b (inc 1)
⌒	M1 R
⌄	M1 L
S	sl1 knitwise
S	sl1 purlwise
⧅	ssk
⧄	k2tog
X	BO
□	k on RS, p on WS
—	p on RS, k on WS
○	YO
△	sl2 knitwise, k1, p2 sso

1. With orange, make 1 center, foll Center Chart.

2. With pink, make 5 small petals, foll Small Petal Chart.

3. With pink, make 8 large petals, foll Large Petal Chart.

4. With pink, make a 4-st knitted cord approx 21" long.

5. With yellow, make a bobble: CO 8 sts, leaving a 12" yarn tail at beg of CO. Work back and forth in St st for 10 rows. Break yarn, leaving a 12" tail. Thread tail through tapestry needle. Run needle through live sts, then sew running sts around rem 3 sides of piece. Wind yarn tail from CO into a ball small enough to fit inside piece (wrap around one finger).

Place yarn tail ball on WS of piece. Pull working end with tapestry needle to snug bobble around filling. Fasten securely to underside of bobble. Make 2nd bobble to match. Sew bobbles to ends of knitted cord.

FINISHING

1. Weave in all ends and block hat and appliqué pieces.

2. Lay center piece flat with right side up. Roll from left to right, keeping lower edge straight. Sew through all layers to hold in place.

3. With RS facing rose center, sew small petals one at a time to rose center. Keep straight lower edges even, and overlap petals.

4. With RS facing backs of small petals, sew large petals one at a time to flower unit. Keep straight lower edges even, and overlap petals.

5. Try on hat or place on hat form. Pin rose in place. Sew rose to hat, stitching all the way around its base.

6. Pin 3 large leaves and 1 small leaf in place as desired, tucking lower edges under rose petals as shown. Sew in place invisibly, tacking in several places to keep them from flopping forward too much.

7. Form cord into a bow shape and pin to hat. Sew in place. Place last small leaf on top of bow, tucking leaf edge under adjacent rose petal. Sew in place.

TIP

Don't actually tie the cord into a bow; a center knot creates too much bulk. Instead, form the loops, cross the ends, and sew in the center to hold securely.

Rose Garden Cloche Schematic

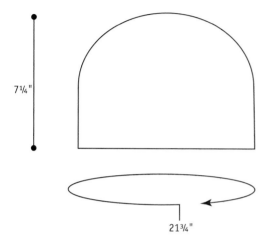

7¼"

21¾"

Flora Cardigan

This cardigan began with a collection of vintage shell buttons purchased at an estate sale. Sumptuous cashmere-blend yarn in soft hues is the perfect backdrop for their pearly luster. Inspired by the embroidered sweaters of the 1940s, Flora's embellishment is a simple combination of chain, daisy, and leaf stitches, highlighted by French knots. Dainty cables and tipped ribbing add interest to Flora's edges.

Specifications

Finished chest measurement: 37¾ (40¾, 42¼, 43¾)"

YARN
DK-weight yarn

Shown: Knit Picks *Capra*, 85% merino wool, 15% cashmere, 123 yd.

MC: Sea Spray (turquoise), 9 (9, 10, 11) balls

CC1: Harbor (teal), 1 ball

CC2: Hunter (dark green), 1 ball

CC3: Honey (gold), 1 ball

CC4: Carnation (pink), 1 ball

CC5: Tiger Lily (orange), 1 ball

GAUGE
22 sts and 34 rows = 4" in main body patt

NEEDLES
Size 5 (3.75mm) 24" circular, or size needed to achieve gauge

NOTIONS
Stitch holders

Tapestry needle

40–60 shell buttons in assorted sizes for embellishment

Nine ½" buttons for placket

Flora Cardigan Charts

CABLE EDGING/PLACKET CHART

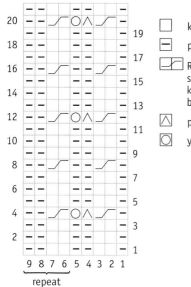

	k on RS, p on WS
—	p on RS, k on WS
⟋⟍	RC (right cross): K 2nd st on left needle, then k 1st st, then drop both sts from left needle
∧	p2tog
○	yo

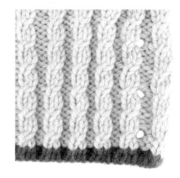

NOTE: Work buttonholes on right placket only

MAIN BODY CHART

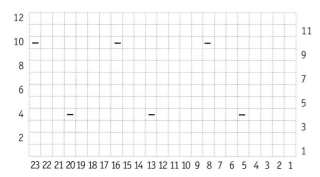

Directions

WORK BODY TO ARMHOLE

1 With CC1, CO 208 (224, 232, 240) sts. Next row (RS): P1, *k2, p2; rep from * to last 3 sts, k2, p1. Work 2 more rows in rib patt. Change to MC and purl 1 WS row. Work rows 1–20 of Cable Edging/Placket Chart. Cont in cable patt (without buttonholes) until piece measures 3" from CO, ending with a WS row. Cont working 8 sts at each end of every row in cable patt for plackets. Work all other sts in Main Body patt. Work even until piece measures 8 (8, 8½, 8½)" from CO, ending with a WS row. Work 2nd set of three buttonholes on right placket.

2 Work even until piece measures 11½ (11½, 12, 12)" from CO, ending with a WS row.

SHAPE ARMHOLES

1 Next row (RS): Work 47 (50, 51, 52) sts in patt, BO 10 (12, 14, 16) sts, work 94 (100, 102, 104) sts in patt, BO 10 (12, 14, 16) sts, work to end of row—47 (50, 51, 52) sts for each front, 94 (100, 102, 104) sts for back.

2 Cont working on left front only. Work 1 WS row. Dec row (RS): K3, ssk, work in patt to end of row. Rep dec row every RS row 7 more times—39 (42, 43, 44) sts.

3 Work even until left front measures 17 (17, 18, 18)" from CO, ending with a RS right cross row.

SHAPE NECKLINE AND SHOULDER

1 Next row (WS): Work 8 sts and place these sts on a holder, BO next 4 (6, 7, 8) sts, work to end of row— 27 (28, 28, 28) sts. BO 3 (4, 4, 4) sts at beg of next WS row—24 sts.

2 Next row (RS): *Work in patt to last 5 sts, k2tog, k3. Rep last row every RS row 5 more times—18 sts.

3 BO 6 sts at beg of next 3 RS rows—no sts.

4 Rejoin working yarn to right front, beg with a WS row. Work as for left front, reversing shaping, and working a set of two buttonholes beg when piece measures 15½ (15½, 16½, 16½)" from CO.

WORK BACK

1 Rejoin working yarn to back, beg with a WS row. Work 1 WS row. Next row (RS): *K3, ssk, work in patt to last 5 sts, k2tog, k3. Rep last row every RS row 7 more times—78 (84, 86, 88) sts. Work even until back measures 17¾ (17¾, 18¾, 18¾)" from CO, ending with a WS row.

2 Next row (RS): Work 22 sts in patt, BO 34 (40, 42, 44) sts, work in patt to end—22 sts each side.

3 Cont working on left back only. Work 1 WS row. Next row (RS): *K3, ssk, work in patt to end of row. Rep last row every RS row 3 more times—18 sts.

4 BO 6 sts at beg of next 3 WS rows—no sts.

5 Rejoin working yarn to right back, beg with a WS row. Work as for left back, reversing shaping.

WORK SLEEVES

1 With CC1, CO 80 (80, 84, 84) sts. Next row (RS): P1, *k2, p2; rep from * to last 3 sts, k2, p1. Work 2 more rows in rib. Change to MC and purl 1 WS row. Work in cable patt (omitting buttonholes) until piece measures 3" from CO, ending with a WS row.

2 Work rows 1–12 of Main Body Chart, dec 20 sts evenly across Row 1—60 (60, 64, 64) sts. Cont in patt, inc 1 st at each end of next row, then every 14th row 7 more times—76 (76, 80, 80) sts. Work even in patt until piece measures 17½ (18,18½, 19)" from CO, ending with a WS row.

3 BO 6 sts at beg of next 2 rows—64 (64, 68, 68) sts. Dec 1 st at each end of next 8 RS rows—48 (48, 52, 52) sts. Work even until piece measures 22 (22½, 23, 23½)" from CO, ending with a WS row. Dec 1 st at each end of next 4 RS rows—40 (40, 44, 44) sts. BO 5 sts at beg of next 8 rows—0 (0, 4, 4) sts. BO.

FINISHING

1 Block pieces.

2 Work embroidery as shown, foll Flora patt, inverting patt on upper left front and center back.

3 Sew shoulder seams.

4 Sew sleeve seams.

5 With RS facing, MC, and working along neck edge, work 8 held placket sts in patt, pick up and knit 108 (116, 120, 124) sts along neck edge, work 8 held placket sts in patt—124 (132, 136, 140) sts. Next row (WS): K1, *p2, k2; rep from * to last 3 sts, p2, k1. Work rows 3–7 of Cable Edging/Placket Chart, including buttonhole on right front. Change to CC1 and work 2 rows in k2, p2 rib. BO in patt.

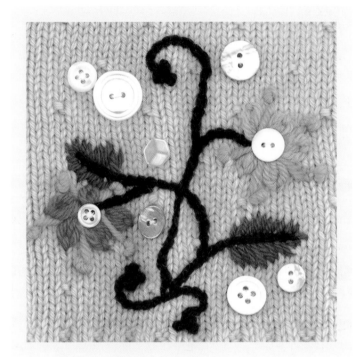

6 Sew sleeves into armholes.

7 Sew embellishment buttons in place as shown.

8 Sew placket buttons in place, under buttonholes.

9 Steam embroidery lightly to block.

Flora Cardigan Embroidery Pattern

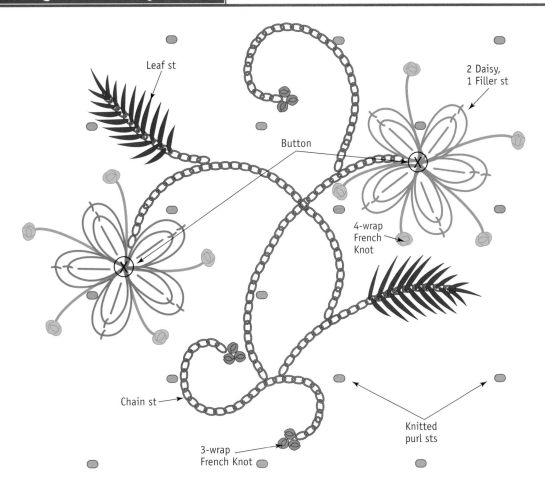

Leaf st

2 Daisy,
1 Filler st

Button

4-wrap
French
Knot

Chain st

Knitted
purl sts

3-wrap
French Knot

Flora Cardigan Schematic

BODY

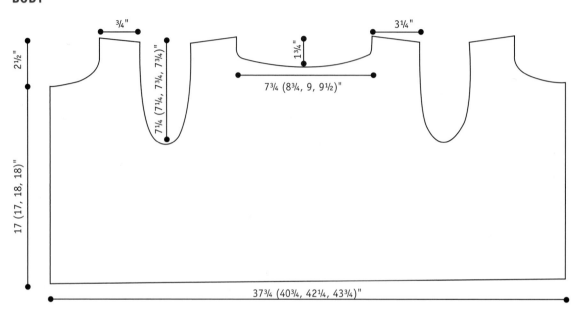

SLEEVE

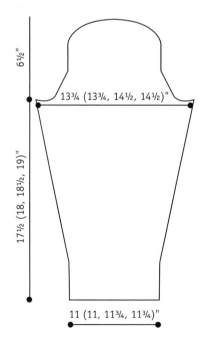

Hook, Line, and Sinker Handbag

Something's definitely fishy. Here's a fun way to showcase a single skein of luxury knitting yarn: Knit a handbag with a great big mouth! The gorgeous, delicate colors in this hand-dyed yarn are derived exclusively from natural dye-stuffs. A combination of rare Polwarth wool and decadent Tussah silk lends a touch of sophistication to this whimsical piece.

Specifications

SIZE
Finished measurements: 17" long x 9½" wide

YARN
DK-weight yarn

Shown: Sincere Sheep *Luminous,* 85% Polwarth wool/15% Tussah silk, 320 yd./4 oz.

MC: Quercus (green), 1 skein

CC1: Tendril (yellow-green), 1 skein

CC2: Modern Alchemy (blue), 1 skein

CC3: Be Mine (pink), 1 skein

GAUGE
26 sts and 36 rnds = 4" in St st

NEEDLES
Size 3 (3.25 mm) 16" circular and DPNs, or size needed to achieve gauge

NOTIONS
4 stitch markers

Stitch holders

Tapestry needle

5¼" purse frame

15" purse chain handle

½ yd. lining fabric

239

Directions

WORK MOUTH PIECES

1 With MC, CO 19 sts. Working back and forth in St st, work 2 rows. Work 10 more rows, incr 1 st at each end of every RS row—29 sts.

2 Work incs on every RS row as foll:

3 Row 1: K1, M1R, k3, M1R, k21, M1L, k3, M1L, k1—33 sts.

4 Row 3: K1, M1R, k6, M1R, k19, M1L, k6, M1L, k1—37 sts.

5 Row 5: K1, M1R, k9, M1R, k17, M1L, k9, M1L, k1—41 sts.

6 Row 7: K1, M1R, k12, M1R, k15, M1L, k12, M1L, k1—45 sts.

7 Row 9: K1, M1R, k15, M1R, k13, M1L, k15, M1L, k1—49 sts.

8 Row 11: K1, M1R, k18, M1R, k11, M1L, k18, M1L, k1—53 sts.

9 Break yarn and place sts on holder. Make 2nd mouth piece to match.

JOIN PIECES AND CONTINUE HEAD

1 Place sts of both mouth pieces on circular needle or DPNs, PM, and join for working in rnds—106 sts. Work 1 rnd even.

2 Resume incs on every other rnd as foll:

3 Rnd 1: K1, M1R, k21, M1R, k9, M1L, k21, M1L, k2, M1R, k21, M1R, k9, M1L, k21, M1L, k1—114 sts.

4 Rnd 3: K1, M1R, k24, M1R, k7, M1L, k24, M1L, k2, M1R, k24, M1R, k7, M1L, k24, M1L, k1—122 sts.

5 Rnd 5: K1, M1R, k27, M1R, k5, M1L, k27, M1L, k2, M1R, k27, M1R, k5, M1L, k27, M1L, k1—130 sts.

6 Rnd 7: K1, M1R, k30, M1R, k3, M1L, k30, M1L, k2, M1R, k30, M1R, k3, M1L, k30, M1L, k1—138 sts.

7 Work 1 rnd even.

WORK BODY

1 Next rnd: *K1, ssk, k30, M1R, k3, M1L, k30, k2tog, k1; rep from * once more. Work 1 rnd even. Rep last 2 rnds until piece measures 7" from CO. Work 2 rnds even. Set-up rnd: K34, PM, k35, PM, k34, PM, k35.

2 Next rnd: K1, ssk, knit to 2 sts before M, k2tog, k1, ssk, work to 3 sts before M, k2tog, k2, ssk, knit to 2 sts before M, k2tog, k1, ssk, knit to last 3 sts, k2tog, k1. Work 3 rnds even. Rep last 4 rnds 11 more times—42 sts. Next rnd: *K1, ssk, knit to M, k1, ssk, knit to 3 sts before M, k2tog, k1; rep from * once more—36 sts.

CLOSE BODY

1 Next rnd: K9. Place 18 sts on each of 2 DPNs.

2 Holding DPNs parallel, work 1 row in k1, p1 rib, working each st through 1 st from each DPN—18 sts.

WORK TAIL FINS

1 With CC1, work 2 rows in k1, p1 rib.

2 Cont in patt, inc 1 st at each end of next 6 RS rows—30 sts.

3 Divide for tail fins as foll: Next row: Work 15 sts, turn. Cont working in rib on 1 side of tail only. Next row: Dec 1, work to last st, inc 1. Work 1 row even. Rep last 2 rows 3 more times. Inc at each end of every 4th row 3 times—21 sts. Dec 1 st at each end of every RS row 9 times—3 sts. Next row: Sl1, k2tog, psso—1 st. Break yarn and pull through last st.

4 Make opposite tail fin, reversing shaping.

WORK SIDE FINS

1 Holding piece with tail up, measure up 3½" from corner of mouth opening. With CC1, pick up and knit 10 sts, centered on side shaping, as shown. Work 1 row in k1, p1 rib. Inc 1 st at each end of next row. Rep last 2 rows 5 more times—22 sts. Work 4 rows even in patt. Dec 1 st at each end of next 2 RS rows—18 sts. BO in patt.

2 Make 2nd fin on opposite side of body to match.

WORK DORSAL FIN

1 Holding piece with tail on right, measure 2" away from tail fin. With CC1, pick up and knit 42 sts along top of fish, ending about 1" before beg of triangle on fish's face. Work short rows to shape fin as foll:

2 Row 1: Sl1, *k1, p1; rep from * to last st, k1.

3 Row 2: Sl1, work in patt to last 5 sts, wrap & turn.

4 Row 3: Sl1, work in patt to last 7 sts, wrap & turn.

5 Row 4: Sl1, work 26 sts in patt, wrap & turn.

6 Row 5: Sl1, work 19 sts in patt, wrap & turn.

7 Row 6: Sl1, work 16 sts in patt, wrap & turn.

8 Row 7: Sl1, work 13 sts in patt, wrap & turn.

9 Row 8: Sl1, work 10 sts in patt, wrap & turn.

10 Row 9: Sl1, work 7 sts in patt, wrap & turn.

11 Row 10: Sl1, work 4 sts in patt, wrap & turn.

12 Row 11: Sl1, work in patt to end, picking up wrap from prior row and working tog with st at each gap, turn.

⑬ Row 12: Sl1, work in patt to end, picking up wrap from prior row and working tog with st at each rem gap, turn.

⑭ BO loosely in patt.

WORK LOWER FINS

❶ With CC1, pick up and knit 7 sts at end of head shaping, as shown. Work in k1, p1 rib, inc at each end of every RS row 3 times—13 sts. Dec 1 st at each end of every 4th row 5 times—3 sts. Next row: Sl1, k2tog, psso—1 st. Break yarn and thread tail through last st.

❷ Make 2nd fin on opposite side to match.

WORK SCALES

Place scales randomly, alternating CC1, CC2, and CC3 as desired. For each scale, holding piece with tail up, pick up and knit 9 sts. Work in garter st for 9 rows. Next 3 RS rows: ssk, knit to last 2 sts, k2tog—3 sts. BO.

FINISHING

❶ Embroider eyes, as shown. Weave in ends at edges of all fins and scales. Wherever possible, pull ends to inside of body and trim to approx 2" long.

❷ Block piece, laying flat with mouth open and tail flat. Check to be sure scales on underside of piece are lying flat, in the same direction. Turn piece over occasionally during drying.

❸ Lay piece flat on top of folded lining fabric. Trace around piece, adding a ¼" seam allowance. Cut out lining (2 pieces) along tracing line.

❹ With RS tog, stitch sides of lining, leaving tail open. Press seams open.

❺ Place purse inside lining, with RS tog, matching lining seams to mouth centers. Pin edges tog along mouth opening. Stitch lining and purse tog with a ¼" seam allowance.

❻ Carefully turn piece RS out through tail opening in lining. Stitch lining closed. Push lining inside bag. Gently press mouth edge with lining fabric facing up, toward iron.

❼ Sew mouth edge into purse frame, easing in fullness as needed. Attach chain handle.

Hook, Line, and Sinker Handbag Schematic

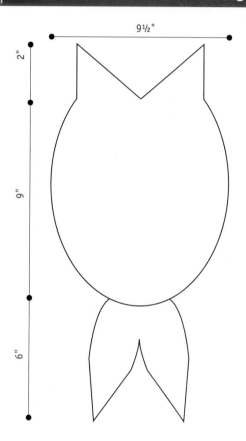

9½"

2"

9"

6"

NOTE: The opening size of the mouth is determined by the purse frame after the knitting is sewn (eased) into it.

PICOT HEM

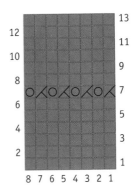

- ☐ k on RS, p on WS
- Ⓞ yo
- ⊠ k2tog

LACE EDGING

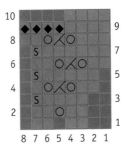

- ☐ k every st, every row
- Ⓞ yo
- ■ no stitch
- ⊠ k2tog
- S slip pwise wyif
- ◆ BO

CABLE & RIB

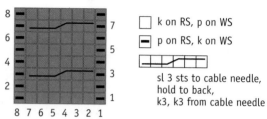

k on RS, p on WS

p on RS, k on WS

sl 3 sts to cable needle,
hold to back,
k3, k3 from cable needle

① CO 8 sts.

② Rep rows 1–8 of cable and rib chart to desired length.

HELIX

❶ CO 20 sts.

❷ Knit into front and back of every st—40 sts.

❸ Purl 1 row.

❹ Knit into front and back of every st—80 sts.

❺ Purl 1 row.

❻ BO loosely (use needle 2 sizes larger).

❼ Coil helix into a spiral and steam to block.

TASSEL

1. Wrap yarn around cardboard 20 times.

2. Thread tapestry needle with 12" of yarn and tie top of tassel snugly. Remove needle, leaving tie to attach to work.

3. Cut ends of yarn and remove from cardboard.

4. Thread tapestry needle with 18" of yarn and wrap around tassel 6–10 times, snugly. Tie knot in wrap yarn and bury end inside tassel.

5. Trim tassel ends evenly.

6. Attach to work.

DAHLIA

1 CO 20 sts, leaving 12" tail.

2 BO 16 sts, knit to end—4 sts.

3 K4, turn. CO 16 sts using cable CO—20 sts.

4 Rep steps 2–3 29 more times.

5 Coil strip of strands snugly tog, stitching in a spiral with CO tail threaded through needle.

CLEMATIS

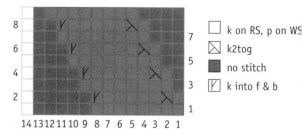

☐	k on RS, p on WS
⊠	k2tog
■	no stitch
Ⅴ	k into f & b

❶ With color A, CO 8 sts. Work Rows 1–8 of chart once. BO. Work 5 more petals in the same manner.

❷ Stitch petals together at points, pinching each in center.

❸ With color B, embroider clustered French knots in flower center as shown.

KNITTED-IN BEADS

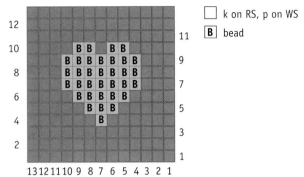

k on RS, p on WS

B bead

① Prestring beads onto yarn.

② For each bead symbol indicated on the chart, slide a bead down the working strand so that it ends up on the RS facing leg of the knit st.

CHAIN STITCH

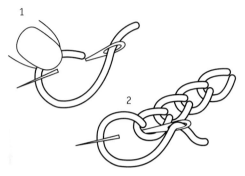

1 The first stitch of the chain is a loop. It starts and stops in the same place.

2 Start the second stitch at the top of the first loop. All the loop stitches are made in the same way.

DOUBLE DAISY

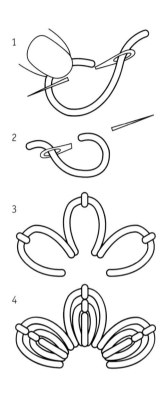

① Make the first stitch the same as for a chain.

② Make a short anchor stitch at the top of the loop.

③ Make additional loops with anchor stitches for each daisy "petal."

④ Layer smaller loops inside the larger loops.

FRENCH KNOT

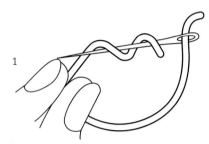

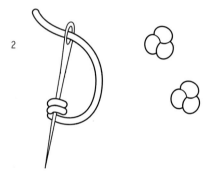

① The knot stitch starts and stops in the same place.

② Wrap the yarn around the needle twice, then pull needle to WS of work, forming knot.

LEAF STITCH

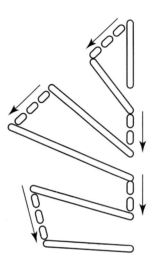

The dotted lines indicate the path of the working strand on the WS of the work. The lines are straight, rather than curved, because the lines of stitching here are straight, rather than curved.

CHAPTER 10

Enhance Your Color Knitting Skills

The techniques outlined in this chapter are used specifically in color knitting, and are often transferrable to other types of knitting. If a particular technique is referenced in one of the projects in this book, here is the place to find it.

Machine Steeks

Before cutting a piece of knitted fabric, secure the knitted stitches around the planned cut using a sewing machine.

MEASURE AND MARK FOR ARMHOLE STEEKS

Armhole steeks are simply straight slots cut into the sides of the completed body tube. Measure the tops of your completed sleeve tubes, and then mark the armholes to the same depth with waste yarn, as shown at right.

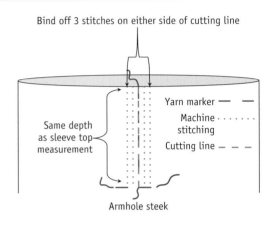

Bind off 3 stitches on either side of cutting line

Yarn marker — —
Machine · · · · · · · ·
stitching
Cutting line — — —

Same depth as sleeve top measurement

Armhole steek

MEASURE AND MARK FOR NECKLINE CURVES

Place waste yarn markers for your neckline curve as shown at right, measuring the neckline depth specified in your pattern, down from the top (1), then across the bottom (2), and then diagonally across the corner (3).

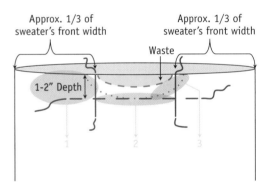

Approx. 1/3 of sweater's front width

Approx. 1/3 of sweater's front width

Waste

1-2" Depth

MARK FOR CENTER FRONT OPENINGS

Place a yarn marker directly down the middle of your center front steek, as shown at right.

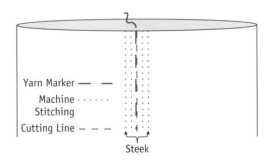

Yarn Marker — —
Machine · · · · · ·
Stitching
Cutting Line — — —

Steek

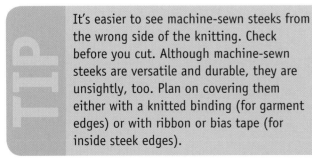

TIP

It's easier to see machine-sewn steeks from the wrong side of the knitting. Check before you cut. Although machine-sewn steeks are versatile and durable, they are unsightly, too. Plan on covering them either with a knitted binding (for garment edges) or with ribbon or bias tape (for inside steek edges).

258

MACHINE STITCH: INSIDE PASSES

With the machine set to a medium-length straight stitch, sew down the center of each column of stitches adjoining the yarn marker.

MACHINE STITCH: OUTSIDE PASSES

Sew another set of 2 stitching lines down the column of stitches 2 columns away from the first.

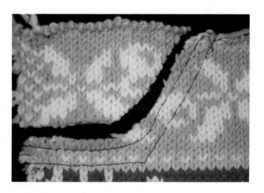

CUT ON MARKING LINES

Slice vertically through the waste yarn marker with sharp sewing shears.

CUT NECKLINE CURVES

Cut the neckline curves close to the 2nd row of machine stitching, following the curve.

Crochet Steeks

Secure the edges of your knitted fabric using a single crochet of fingering-weight yarn. Crochet steeks do not need to be covered, so they are perfect for openings adjoining ribbed edges.

MARK FOR CUTTING LINES

Place waste yarn markers for each cutting line. The marker must go down the center of a single column of knitted stitches rather than in the valley between two columns.

SET UP FOR SINGLE CROCHET

1 With hook, pull a loop from back of work to front, through lower edge of steek.

2 Catch 2nd loop around edge of work and pull through 1st loop.

TIP

Crochet steeks work only on untreated (non-superwash) 100% wool. They will pull out of knitting made from any other type of yarn. Machine-sewn steeks should be used for non-wool or superwash projects.

Once you pick up and knit edgings adjacent to crochet steeks, their edges will automatically fold back and away, toward the wrong side of the garment. Washing and wearing actually makes crochet steeks stronger.

① Pass hook under 1 leg of each st of the 2-st column adjoining waste yarn marker.

② Wrap working yarn over hook and pull 2nd loop through.

③ Wrap working yarn again and pull 3rd loop through prior 2 loops already on hook.

④ Repeat steps 1–3 without skipping any knitted sts. Break crochet yarn, pulling tail through last crochet loop. Work a 2nd row of single crochet on opposite side of waste yarn marker. Slice vertically through marker line, between the 2 columns of single crochet.

Knitted Hems

A knitted hem offers the advantage of full elasticity to a polished garment edge without pulling it in toward the body. A knitted hem has three parts: the facing, a turning ridge, and the actual hem. On the last row of the hem, you pick up a loop from the knitted cast-on and knit through it.

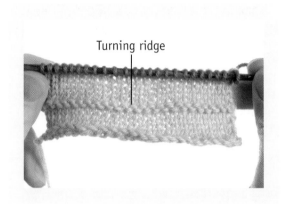

Turning ridge

1. After folding hem to WS, place right needle through first st, then through first loop of knitted CO.

2. Wrap working yarn, then pull new st through the old one and the CO loop.

1

2

3. Rep steps 1 and 2 without skipping any sts or CO loops. Check right side of work often to make sure hem isn't slanting from having missed a CO loop.

Working the joining row with a needle one size larger than that used for the main body of the work helps avoid an unsightly "fold line" from forming on the right side of the work.

RS

WS

Sometimes referred to as I-cord ("idiot cord"), knitted cord is one of the most versatile items you can knit. Use it for ties, straps, appliqués, or edges.

1 Using DPN, CO required number of sts. Knitted cord can be worked in any gauge and with any number of sts, depending on the thickness or fineness of the cord required. This example uses 5 sts.

2 Knit all sts. At end of row, rather than turning work, slide knitted sts to opposite end of needle, draw working yarn across back of work snugly, and then knit all the sts again.

3 Cont knitting and sliding until you have made the length of cord you need. Break working yarn and thread through tapestry needle. Thread yarn tail through all live sts and pull snugly to close. Pull tail through inside of cord to hide it.

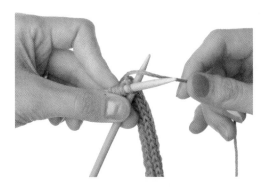

Reading Charts

Many color knitting techniques call for you to follow charts, either in addition to or in lieu of written instructions. Once you are comfortable with them, charted instructions can be more intuitive than written ones.

KNITTING FLAT

Begin at the bottom of the chart and work toward the top. For flat knitting (back and forth, in rows), read each line from right to left on the right-side rows and from left to right on the wrong-side rows.

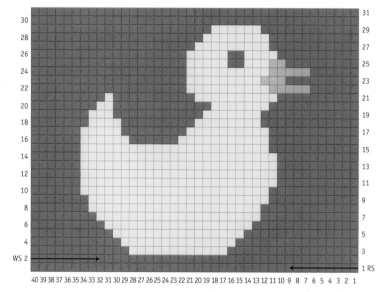

CIRCULAR KNITTING

Begin at the bottom of the chart and work toward the top. For circular knitting (in the round), read every line from the right to the left, repeating at the end of each motif, until you have worked all the stitches for the round. Begin again on the right side of the next row up on the chart for the next round.

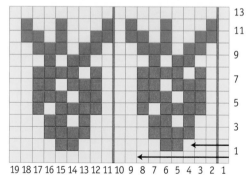

TIP

When reading charts, adhesive notes and reusable tape are helpful to keep track of which row you are working. Always cover the rows at the top of the chart (those you have not yet worked).

Button Loops

When spacing, the size of a closure, or garment construction won't permit a regular buttonhole, button loops can save the day.

SETUP FOR LOOP

1 Bring double-threaded tapestry needle out through edge.

2 Make a long st, slightly longer than the diameter of your button. Bring needle through edge of work, then out again at beg of loop.

1

2

3 Bring needle under base strands, from front to back, without pulling it all the way through.

4 Pass needle through working loop.

3

4

5 Pull covering st snug.

6 Rep steps 1–3 until all base strands are covered. Thread tail back through last few sts to hide, trimming close to loop.

6

These inexpensive yarn-covered buttons are not only fun and easy to make, but also match your knitting exactly.

① Leaving a tail about 6" long, cover a plastic ring with sts as for making a button loop. Once ring is completely covered, twist sts to inside of ring so bumps are on the inside and smooth wraps are on the outside.

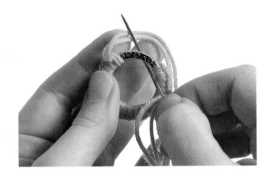

② Wrap working strands around outside of ring 4 times, creating 8 spokes. Spokes will look even on front and uneven on back. Make a st around the center of the spokes, from back to front, evening spokes out on the back.

③ Bring needle up to the left of a spoke, then down to the right of it. Now go up and down around next spoke to the left, and so on, counterclockwise.

④ Cont weaving around spokes until they are completely covered. Tie off end. Weave in yarn tails.

Possibly the worst cast-on for the finished edge of a garment, the loose and loopy nature of the knitted cast-on makes it the perfect choice when you are planning to knit in a hem.

① Make a slipknot and place it on your left needle.

② Knit slipknot "stitch," but do not slip it off left needle. Instead, place new st back on left needle next to it.

1

2

③ Cont knitting through each consecutive st and placing resulting new st back on left needle, until all sts are CO.

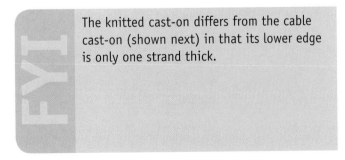

FYI

The knitted cast-on differs from the cable cast-on (shown next) in that its lower edge is only one strand thick.

Cable Cast-On

In addition to forming a firm, durable edge, the cable cast-on is useful in other situations, such as when you are adding new areas of stitches to existing knitting (like a steek) or working modular units.

1 Begin by placing a slipknot on your left needle.

2 Holding tail from slipknot firmly with your left hand, place right needle to left side of slipknot and wrap working yarn around it. Place resulting new st on left needle, next to slipknot.

3 For next and remaining consecutive sts, place right needle between last st and the one prior. Wrap yarn, make new st, and place it on left needle.

④ Cont until all sts are CO.

The cable cast-on is more durable and attractive than the knitted cast-on; it results in an edge with two strands rather than one.

Three-Needle Bind-Off

This technique joins any two sets of live stitches into a secure and bulk-free seam. Worked from the wrong side, it's nearly invisible. From the right side, it becomes a design element.

---

1 Place 2 sets of live sts on needles. Hold knitting RS tog for WS seam or WS tog for RS seam. Hold pieces to be joined in your left hand.

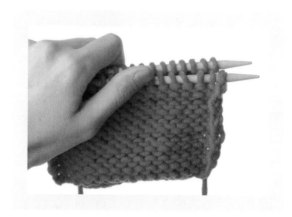

2 With your right hand, insert 3rd needle through each of the first sts on both needles. Wrap working yarn, then pull new st through both old ones.

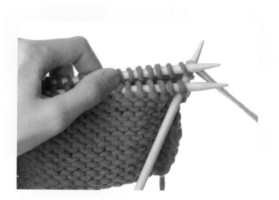

3 Work next st from each needle tog, then pass first st over 2nd on right needle to BO.

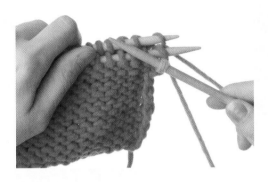

4 Cont until all sts from both pieces are worked. Break working strand and pull tail through last loop.

TIP

The three-needle bind-off works only when the two pieces to be joined contain the exact same number of live stitches.

Crochet Seams

Similar to the three-needle bind-off, the crochet seam joins two pieces of knitting, but without the need for live stitches.

---

1. In your left hand, hold 2 pieces of knitting with RS together for a WS (invisible) seam or with WS together for a RS (decorative) seam.

2. With a slipknot of working yarn already on hook, pull a loop from back of work to front, through edges of both pieces.

3. Reach around the edge of the piece with the hook, catch the yarn, and pull through both loops on the hook.

4. Pull a loop from back of work to front, through edges of both pieces.

5. Wrap yarn around hook, creating a 3rd loop. Pull 3rd loop through the 1st and 2nd.

6. Rep steps 4 and 5 until both edges are joined. Break yarn and pull though last loop to secure.

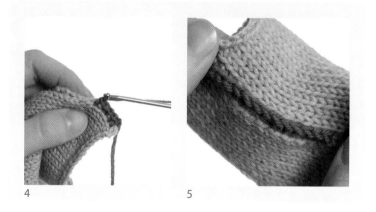

A ny time you need to join two strands of the same color, a wet splice (also called a *split splice*) can do it invisibly.

---

① Tease the plies of the yarn apart and break off half of them (or just one, if your yarn is 3-ply), on both the end of the old strand and the end of the new one.

② Wet both strands in your mouth, then overlap them in the palm of your left hand.

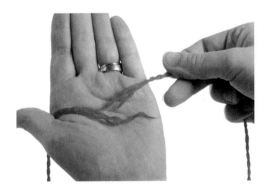

③ Placing your left hand atop the right, rub the strands briskly together until you feel them heat up and begin to dry.

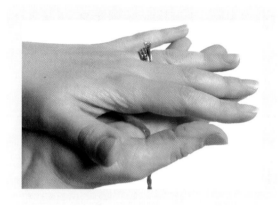

A properly felted wet splice is invisible on both sides of the knitted fabric and is stronger than either original strand.

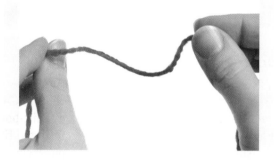

TIP

The wet splice works only on untreated (non-superwash) 100% wool and other felt-able yarns. For all other fiber contents, tie overhand knots, then weave in the ends.

Due to its nature of combined strands, color knitting benefits greatly from the final step of blocking. This last bit of effort enables the yarn's fibers to remember their original size and shape, relaxing them into a cohesive fabric. Different blocking techniques work for different fibers, but generally speaking, the more natural fiber in your project, the more water it will need for proper blocking.

WASHING

Give your pieces a warm 20-minute soak in no-rinse wool wash, then gently squeeze out the excess water. Pin them into shape on a flat surface and let them air-dry completely before seaming them together.

SPRITZING

Lay your knitted pieces on a flat surface, then spray liberally with a squirt-bottle filled with water. Once the fibers begin to relax, pin them into place and let them air-dry.

STEAMING

Before or after seams are worked (or both), you can use the lowest steam setting on your iron to gently revive and shape your knitted fabric. Be sure you never rest the weight of the iron directly on the knitted fabric. Let dry completely before moving from the ironing surface.

Appendix

Abbreviations

Abbreviation	Meaning
alt	alternate; alternating
approx	approximately
beg	begin(s); beginning
bet	between
BO	bind off
CO	cast on
cont	continue(s); continuing
dec(s)	decrease(s); decreasing
foll	follow(s); following
inc(s)	increase(s); increasing
incl	including
k	knit
k1b	knit into back of stitch
k2tog	knit 2 stitches together
kfb	knit into front and back of stitch
k tbl	knit through back of loop
kwise	knitwise
LH	left-hand
M1	make one
M1L	make one left
M1R	make one right
p	purl
p1b	purl into back of stitch
p2sso	pass 2 slipped stitches over
p2tog	purl 2 stitches together
patt	pattern
pfb	purl into front and back of stitch
PM	place marker
prev	previous
psso	pass slipped stitch over

Abbreviation	Meaning
p tbl	purl through back of loop
pwise	purlwise
rem	remain(s); remaining
rep	repeat
rev St st	reverse stockinette stitch
RH	right-hand
rnd(s)	round(s)
RS	right side
sk	skip
skp	slip 1 knitwise, knit 1, pass slipped stitch over
sl	slip(ping)
sl st	slip(ped) stitch
ssk	slip, slip, knit
ssp	slip, slip, purl
st(s)	stitch(es)
St st	stockinette stitch
tbl	through back of loop(s)
tog	together
WS	wrong side
wyib	with yarn in back
wyif	with yarn in front
yb	yarn at back
yf	yarn forward
yo	yarn over
*	repeat starting point
( )	alternate measurements and/or instructions
[ ]	instructions that are to be worked as a group the specified number of times

Resource Guide

Abstract Fiber
3676 SE Martins St.
Portland, OR 97202
503-703-1120
www.abstractfiber.com

Black Water Abbey Yarns
P.O. Box 470688
Aurora, CO 80047-0688
720-320-1003
www.abbeyyarns.com

Blue Moon Fiber Arts, Inc.
56587 Mollenhour Rd.
Scappoose, OR 97056
503-922-3431
www.bluemoonfiberarts.com

Crystal Palace Yarns
160 23rd St.
Richmond, CA 94804
www.straw.com

Freia Fine Handpaints
6023 Christie Ave.
Emeryville, CA 94608
www.freiafibers.com

Homestead Heirlooms
Pewaukee, WI
262-352-8738
www.homesteadheirlooms.com

Kauni
Odderbaekvej 13
Fuglsang
7323 Give
Denmark
www.kauni.com

Knit One, Crochet Too
91 Tandberg Trail, Unit 6
Windham, ME 04062
207-892-9625
www.knitonecrochettoo.com

Knit Picks
13118 NE 4th St.
Vancouver, WA 98684
800-574-1323
www.knitpicks.com

Lacis
Museum of Lace and Textiles & Retail Store
2982 Adeline St.
Berkeley, CA 94703
510-843-7290
www.lacis.com

MadelineTosh
7515 Benbrook Pkwy.
Benbrook, TX 76126
817-249-3066
www.madelinetosh.com

Nordic Fiber Arts
4 Cutts Rd.
Durham, NH 03824
603-868-1196
www.nordicfiberarts.com

Noro
K. F. I.
P.O. Box 336
315 Bayview Ave.
Amityville, NY 11701
www.knittingfever.com

Patons
320 Livingstone Ave. South, Box 40
Listowel, ON N4W 3H3
Canada
www.patonsyarns.com

Peace Fleece
475 Porterfield Rd.
Porter, ME 04068
800-482-2841
www.peacefleece.com

The Sanguine Gryphon
7923 B Industrial Park Rd.
Easton, MD 21601
410-770-5557
www.sanguinegryphon.com

Simply Shetland
18375 Olympic Ave. South
Seattle, WA 98188
877-743-8526
www.simplyshetland.net

Simply Socks Yarn Company
1315 E. State Blvd.
Fort Wayne, IN 46805
260-416-2397
www.simplysockyarn.com

Sincere Sheep
Napa Valley, CA
www.sinceresheep.com

Further Reading

Epstein, Nicky. *Knitting on the Edge: Ribs, Ruffles, Lace, Fringes, Flora, Points & Picots*. New York, NY: Sixth & Spring Books, 2004.

Epstein, Nicky. *Knitting Over the Edge: Unique Ribs, Cords, Appliqués, Colors, Nouveau*. New York, NY: Sixth & Spring Books, 2005.

Epstein, Nicky. *Knitting Beyond the Edge: Cuffs & Collars, Necklines, Corners & Edges, Closures*. New York, NY: Sixth & Spring Books, 2006.

Høxbro, Vivian. *Domino Knitting*. Loveland, CO: Interweave Press, 2002.

Huff, Mary Scott. *The New Stranded Colorwork*. Loveland, CO: Interweave Press, 2009.

Luters, Ginger. *Module Magic: Creative Projects to Knit One Block at a Time*. Sioux Falls, SD: XRX Books, 2003.

Montano, Judith Baker. *Elegant Stitches*. Lafayette, CA: C&T Publishing, 1995.

Parkes, Clara. *The Knitter's Book of Yarn*. New York, NY: Potter Craft, 2007.

Radcliffe, Margaret. *The Essential Guide to Color Knitting Techniques*. North Adams, MA: Storey Publishing, 2008.

Stanfield, Lesley. *100 Flowers to Knit & Crochet: A Collection of Beautiful Blooms for Embellishing Garments, Accessories, and More*. New York, NY: St. Martin's Griffin, 2009.

Starmore, Alice. *Alice Starmore's Book of Fair Isle Knitting*. Mineola, NY: Dover Publications, 2009.

Vogue Knitting Stitchionary, Volume 3: Color Knitting. New York, NY: Sixth & Spring Books, 2006.

Walker, Barbara G. *Mosaic Knitting*. Pittsville, WI: Schoolhouse Press, 1997.

Index